IN THE GRANDSTANDS

CHAMPION YOUR TEEN THROUGH THE TEARS AND TRIUMPHS OF SPORT

DR JO LUKINS

FOREWORD BY 3-TIME OLYMPIAN
SUZY BATKOVIC

First published by Ultimate World Publishing 2020
Copyright © 2020 Dr Jo Lukins

ISBN

Paperback - 978-1-922497-08-6
Ebook - 978-1-922497-09-3

Dr Jo Lukins has asserted her right under the Copyright, Designs and Patents Act 1988 to be identified as the author of this work. The information in this book is based on the author's experiences and opinions. The publisher specifically disclaims responsibility for any adverse consequences, which may result from use of the information contained herein. Permission to use information has been sought by the author. Any breaches will be rectified in further editions of the book.

All rights reserved. No part of this publication may be reproduced, stored in or introduced into a retrieval system, or transmitted in any form, or by any means (electronic, mechanical, photocopying, recording or otherwise) without the prior written permission of the author. Any person who does any unauthorised act in relation to this publication may be liable to criminal prosecution and civil claims for damages. Enquiries should be made through the publisher.

Cover design: Ultimate World Publishing
Layout and typesetting: Ultimate World Publishing
Editor: Marinda Wilkinson

Ultimate World Publishing
Diamond Creek,
Victoria Australia 3089
www.writeabook.com.au

PRAISE FOR SPORT

BY THE KIDS

I like sport because playing soccer makes me feel happy. It keeps me active and busy and it's fun to verse my friends.

Addison, 12 years

I enjoy sport as it takes my mind off problems going on in the world. It is fun and enjoyable, especially if you're playing with friends. It also helps with your teamwork as you help each other by pacing each other or trying to win a game of touch.

Angus, 14 years

Sport allows me to meet new people and create friendships and bonds over something we share an interest in. I am able to improve my physical and mental health with people encouraging me to do my best. Playing a sport isn't always about winning or coming first or getting a PB, it's about learning how to work with people, to create a strong team with like-minded people and to encourage each other, especially on the days we don't feel motivated.

Ashleigh, 17 years

I enjoy getting to hang out with my friends, and exercising makes me feel good. Soccer also gives me something to do, and it's a fun sport.

Cadence, 10 years

I have always loved sport even from a young age for a variety of reasons. Sport allows me to keep physically fit and healthy in a fun environment. It also affords me the opportunity to meet new friends, travel to new places and create lifelong memories to look back on.

Connor, 17 years

Sport is fun and keeps you fit – which you need throughout your life. Sport is great because you get to travel and go to awesome places. Playing sport is an easy way to meet new friends. I'm a referee, so I also get to boss adults around!

Dylan, 14 years

My favourite sport is tennis because lots of my friends play it and I'm good at it. Most of my family play tennis, so it's fun for us to play together.

Hannah, 11 years

I enjoy playing hockey because I get to meet new people and go to new places and learn new stuff.

Hunter, 10 years

Sport offers every life skill you need. From building your confidence, how to manage conflict and building teamwork with a group of people. Through sport you can laugh as soon as the competition is done. It's like an escape when the rest of the world gets too serious.

Jayden, 16 years

Community is the driving factor that keeps sport going. Without the local group of friends, family, coaches and officials, my motivation to pursue my sport and to strive for success would not happen. Especially as a referee, we rely on the connections with the team of officials to support and encourage young whistle-blowers to continue to get onto the field each week and have a go. Just like the players, referees experience the highs and the lows of sporting performance, but having a network of people that guide you through these emotions always empower you to strive to be even better next time.

Lachlan, 17 years

I love my sport because you get to meet new friends. It is also fun after school when we train as a team. Sport is fun because it challenges you to improve your skills.

Nicholas, 10 years

I like playing because I get to spend time with my friends. I wasn't very good at tennis when I started, but I like that I'm getting better. I get to play every week, and training with my coach is fun.

Rebecca, 14 years

What I love the most about sport is the ability to be with friends while still keeping active. It's always enjoyable to play with friends and you know it's good for you. It's just always fun.

Reilly, 15 years

My sport is swimming. I've been doing it since I was eight. Because I am a good swimmer it means we can go out in our boat more because Mum and Dad don't worry about me being safe. I love being in the water, its refreshing.

Scarlett, 13 years

CONTENTS

Praise for Sport by the Kids iii
Foreword by Suzy Batkovic..xiii
Prelude: In the Beginning...xvii

Chapter 1: In the Background: Helpful Conversations 1
  discussion points..*3*
  what do the questions you ask say about you? *4*
  motivating mojo *7*
  which type of motivation is better? *8*
  don't pay to play *10*
  fixed mindset vs. performance mindset......................*11*

Chapter 2: In the Process: Effort over Outcome 15
  perfection vs. excellence..*17*
  focusing on personal control *20*
  fear of failure...*22*
  fear of success *27*
  ability, effort and self-esteem...................................*29*

Chapter 3: In the Depths: Managing Disappointment 33
when it goes pear-shaped 34
normalising grief..36
why losing is good for you 38
learning from success 40
process over outcome...41
the curse of the PB 42
when your child says, 'no more'. 44

Chapter 4: In the Mind: Mental Strategies.................47
speaking the lingo...48
your role in the mental game 49
how can you cross the language divide?......................51
the goldilocks principle 53
mental commentary 55
self-efficacy 57
goal setting 60
SMART goals..62
habit formation 65
wysiwyg..68
confidence? check!..72
how a mental skills coach can help 74

Chapter 5: In the Pain: Coping with Injury................77
more than skin-deep...78
the importance of attitude 79
ways to support your teen through injuries 82
returning from injury...85
career over..86

Chapter 6: In the Smile: Keeping it Fun 89
fun comes first 90
fun and dropout 92
fun as an intervention 93
why does fun make a difference? 94
how can you emphasise the value of fun? 96

Chapter 7: In the Heart: Why Gratitude Matters 97
positive benefits of gratitude 99
the mechanism of gratitude 100
self-control and gratitude 101
the power of what you get to do 102
using gratitude to reach goals 104
gratitude in disguise 105
thank you to the opposition 108

Chapter 8: In the Mirror: Leading by Example 109
what sort of parent am I? 111
what was your sporting journey? 113
chip off the old block 114
you as a role model 116
the curious observer 117
your child as a mirror 118
same but different 119
social media trap 121
the roller-coaster of discipline 122
the six words your child needs to hear you say 124
aeroplane safety briefing 125

Chapter 9: On the Sideline: Respect for All 127
    communication is key 129
    when something goes wrong 133
    when you are the coach 135
    be grateful 137

Chapter 10: In the Zone:
The Imbalance of Life and Sport 139
    is balance even possible? 141
    flashback 143
    the rested teen 146
    the electronic drug 149
    strategies for better sleep 151

Chapter 11: In the Wondering: Q & A 153

Chapter 12: In a Nutshell: Ten Key Takeaways 161

Further reading and references 164
About the Author 166
Bonus Offer 169
Need a Speaker for Your Sporting Club? 171
Online Learning 173

To the athletes who have invited me into your lives – it is your stories, journeys, challenges and successes that have made this book possible. I wish you great joy in your sport. Thank you.

To my village – thank you for your never-ending support. It's amazing how far you can go, just because others believe in you.

To Dylan, Lachlan and Joe, once again you have championed me through this project. Thank you for always being the soft place to land. To the moon and back xx

Finally, to the parents of young athletes. I promise I get it. At times it can be tough and we can have questions as to what the best response in a situation is. We can feel tested and wonder if we are making the correct decisions. Please trust that we are all doing the best we can. I hope this book helps to reinforce what already makes sense to you, encourages you to challenge your thinking and provides some of the support we all need to navigate parenting, in the grandstands.

> Making the decision to have a child is momentous. It is to decide forever to have your heart go walking around outside your body.
> **Elizabeth Stone**

FOREWORD

BY SUZY BATKOVIC

WHEN I THINK ABOUT how my parents managed my sport when I was young, I feel very grateful. They never pushed me to do anything. They would ask the question, 'What do you love?' and encourage me to do it. They never yelled on the sidelines and would always find ways to support my brother and I, especially if we were not playing as well as we'd like. If I missed five shots in a row and was struggling, my parents would always be there to help me learn from it and keep going. Mum would say, 'You made a mistake. Why are you worrying about it? It's over. Move on'. When I think about all those years of Mum championing me and telling me to keep my head up and try again, I can clearly see the positive impact it had on my mindset and self-belief. She always made me feel like it was ok to back myself and take the next shot – and that drive and determination to get better and believe in myself has been such an important part of my success as a professional athlete.

Now a parent myself, I'm only just beginning to fully appreciate the efforts of Mum and Dad supporting me from the grandstands.

They were always there to pick up the pieces when things went wrong, but not before they let me experience the challenging moments for myself. This was important, as it allowed me to learn many valuable lessons along the way and to grow in both sport and in life. This is undoubtably one of many difficult balancing acts for parents, and it is one of the valuable topics covered in Dr Jo's book.

As a sports psychologist, Dr Jo has helped countless athletes be their best, from juniors to the elite. She understands the important role a supportive family plays in the journey of a young athlete and how critical it is to laying the foundation of a lifelong love of sport. And while her professional expertise shines through on every page, it's her personal experience of the highs and lows of sport with her own children that adds another level of insight and understanding to the real-life experience of sporting parents.

Whether you're a professional athlete or a child starting out in sport, it's very easy to get caught up internalising the negative. When you've got that positive person in the background, telling you to keep trying and it will come, it's so important, especially in those early days. When I look back now, it was only ever support that my team and I received from my parents. That's what makes this book such an important resource for families at all levels of junior sport. It helps parents understand what they can do to support their kids in sport, no matter their age or ability. And without the unnecessary burden of pressure or expectation.

Dad built a little basketball court at our house for my brother and me. The kids in the neighbourhood would come and play, but most afternoons it was just my brother and I, and every afternoon in those early years he would whoop me. Every single day. But, that didn't stop me from turning up the next day and giving it all I had. Finally, the day came when it was me who got the points on the board. There's no doubt all that streetball we played geared me up for what was to come!

My hope for my daughters is that in sport they may also find their passion. Whatever that sport might be. I want them to experience all the benefits of sport that I found: the teamwork, the health benefits. But most of all, the joy of it. I never want to be 'that parent' screaming from the grandstands. I want to be constructive, to give my kids the space to work out what they want. When I think of our daughters, sure we're there to protect and guide them, but ultimately, they need to work out what they want and navigate their own path.

Sport has the potential to bring so much positivity to a child's life – but in the early years they can't do it alone. For parents wanting to support their kids as they navigate the highs and lows of sport, Dr Jo's book is a valuable companion. The format is perfect for parents short on time to glean the information they need on demand and I know I'll be revisiting my copy regularly over the years as I take my seat in the grandstands.

Suzy Batkovic
October 2020

PRELUDE

IN THE BEGINNING

IN SOME WAYS, THE early years may have seemed more manageable. You dressed them in their oversized uniforms, they looked so little in their boots, perhaps on a court, or standing on the blocks. Did they win? Did they lose? Did they care? Perhaps not if there was an ice block at the end of it all! You cheered from the grandstands or the sideline, hoping they were having fun, and then came back again next week to do it all again.

Sport offers excellent opportunities for our children. Done well, it provides the game plan for raising happy children that learn positive values and teaches essential life lessons. Poorly done, the enjoyment of sport soon disappears, resulting in a generation of adults who are unhappy and unhealthy. A recent review of 557 studies across 30 different sports concluded 70% of teen athletes leave competition by the age of 13. It doesn't have to be this way, and parents hold a crucial role in facilitating the sporting experience of children.

Success leaves clues. This book aims to share the knowledge and lessons for parents to best support their children through their sporting journey. We can all benefit from these lessons. With consideration and implementation of the insights within this book, we can help our children through their sporting journey and enjoy our seat, in the grandstand.

who is this book for?

In writing this book, I know that the readers are parents and caregivers who have hopes for their children's sport that include some or all of the following:
- ⇒ they want what's best for their children through competition
- ⇒ they want their participation in the competition to be fun
- ⇒ they want their child to learn physical skills and tactics
- ⇒ they want their child to perform and succeed at the level of their potential
- ⇒ they want their child to develop a love of a particular sport or physical activity as a lifelong pursuit
- ⇒ they want their child to develop some capabilities, learn life lessons and personal resolve
- ⇒ they want their child to learn skills to navigate the disappointments in life when they come along.

There is also an opportunity for some children to reach absolute excellence in their sport. Whilst it is a small percentage of the population that get there, some athletes will go on to perform at the pinnacle of their sport, and perhaps even make a career from the sport that they love. It certainly won't be the majority. Deriving an income from sport happens for a tiny percentage of the population. Of the top 100 earners in sport in 2019, one was a woman (Serena Williams), ten sports were represented, the average age was 31 years, and Nike sponsored 52 of those athletes. One person in 562,400 have the opportunity to compete at an Olympic Games, and an even smaller 0.0004% of the population will receive a coveted gold medal. Interestingly, one in four parents (around 26%) have aspirations that their child will one day become a professional athlete. I remember discussing this tiny percentage with one teenage athlete. 'Well won't that make it even more awesome when I stand on the podium, Jo!' he remarked. You've got to love optimism!

My assumption in writing this book is that as a parent, you want what's best for your child and are seeking some guidance and support. There is much pressure placed on parents in sport settings, and at times we can feel judged. Parents can be labelled as 'helicopter', 'lawnmower' and even 'fighter pilot'. None of these are flattering. Our children don't arrive with a manual, but in terms of sport, this book certainly hopes to be a guidebook.

who is this book about?

Depending on the sport, our children can be mature athletes at 14 years (if they are a gymnast) or a beginner at 16 years (if they are an aspiring long-distance runner). If this book has found you, it is likely that you have an athlete in the teen years, however, the age may vary around that. Whilst not particularly intended for the young athlete who is in their first year of modified soccer or netball, you could certainly read this book to gain some background to prepare you for the years ahead. We also know that development and maturity vary, so you will know when the information in this book suits your family.

To avoid repetition, I will refer to our young people as a child or teen interchangeably. No matter what their age, they will always be our children! I have been careful not to label your child too often as an athlete, and this has been done deliberately. Your child currently participates in sport. However, you are raising a child, not an athlete. It is important that their identity in sport and as an athlete is part of who they are, but not all of who they are. This will become particularly evident when we get into the discussions around injury, retirement and finishing a sport.

not my finest moment

Sport offers plenty of opportunities to remind ourselves just how human we are! I am here to support you through that journey. When we reflect on our parenting and try as best we can with what we know, we set ourselves up to do it well.

I understand the 'humanity' of parenting as much as anyone and will share a personal story which was certainly not my finest moment (and still makes me cringe). We live in Queensland, Australia, a beautiful part of the world where we have 300 days of sunshine each year. Most homes have swimming pools, and children, therefore, must have competent water skills. Further, swimming is a popular activity for school children in our region. Both of my sons commenced swimming lessons at four months of age, with a key focus being on their ability to be safe in the water. As they got older and their swimming capabilities improved, they moved into swim squads a few times a week, an activity that they both enjoyed.

One day, my (then) eight-year-old announced at school pick up that he didn't want to go to training that afternoon. My belief is sport provides our children with an opportunity to learn the importance of reliably keeping a commitment. I decided on this afternoon that this was one of those times. Tuesday afternoon is swim squad; therefore, we go – even on the days we don't want to.

My son, however, was adamant that he was not going to swim. Memory fails me as to how I convinced him to put his swimmers on, but I recall walking onto the pool deck with him still protesting that he wasn't going to get in the water. I changed tactics and told him that the decision was his. However, he had to be responsible to say to the coach that he did not intend to train. Possibly my strategy was that he would back out of that conversation, or the coach would talk him into the session.

He walked to the coach, the coach greeted him, and mortified, I watched my son inform the coach that he wouldn't be training (you will recall, precisely as I told him to). I interrupted (please note my cringing has begun) and said to him that he would be training. My son told me that he wouldn't, and the coach watched as the conversation went back and forth between my son and me, like a tennis match. Ok, not really a conversation, more like an argument by this stage.

I am now pausing my typing to continue this story from under my desk! Not satisfied with the outcome and my child doing what I had told him would be ok, I picked my son up, held him over the water, and as the coach watched on in horror, dropped my child into the water. He came up spluttering, both shocked and embarrassed that I did this to him in front of the entire squad. The coach looked at me his mouth wide open, pointed to the far side of the pool, and said 'Jo, how about you go over there and take a seat'.

It felt a long walk to the other side of the pool. I wished I had a Tardis that could go back in time and restart my afternoon from the moment my son walked out of school. In that half-hour, I held a fixed view as to what needed to happen, was not seeing the world from my sons' point of view, and even if I wanted the outcome to be different my choice of managing it was not ideal. In a nutshell, that is parenting. Some days we get it right, some days we try, and it doesn't come out the way we hope, or we rethink our thoughts or actions, and they come up short. I certainly understand what it is to make mistakes as a parent. Therefore, this book offers you information and strategies based on the research and evidence of psychological science and the wisdom I have gained from years of working with families and coaches in sporting settings. None of us is perfect, and thankfully that is not what we need to aim for: good-enough will do.

In case you are wondering how our afternoon at the pool finished up, permit me to finish the story. The coach had a conversation with my son. Something along the lines that he understood that he didn't want to train, and he thought Mum needed some fresh air. She had probably had a long day (!), and that my son could decide whether he wanted to return to Mum, be an assistant coach for the afternoon or he could get in the water with his friends. Not surprisingly, my son declined the option to return to me! For about five minutes, he walked the pool deck with the coach, holding the stopwatch and the coach pointing out instructional tips for my son based on the other swimmers. The coach then set a drill that my son particularly liked and next thing you know he was in the water, swimming with the group. I am so grateful to the coach. At the moment it was needed, he allowed my son to feel heard, empathised with how I might be feeling, gave my son options and the power to make decisions and then gently guided him back to what he was ready to do. A later conversation between my son and I, including an apology from myself, allowed us to continue the afternoon in better shape.

I deliberated about sharing this story with you, primarily because it may not cast me in a positive light! Ego is a funny thing. However, I often think back to an insightful quote, by an Australian soldier, Cpl Matt Williams who said, 'A good day is a good day, and a bad day is a great story'. I'm still to find that Tardis, so the afternoon at the pool will remain a part of my parenting history. I have decided now that it is a teachable moment to recognise that well-meaning parents make mistakes, and that is more than ok. For the record, my son (now 14 years old) tells me he has no recollection of the afternoon at the pool!

read on the run

One of the most precious commodities that we have is time. In writing this book, I've been mindful of the many things parents need to include in any given day. Often parents don't necessarily have the time to read as much as they would like to. Therefore, this book has been designed to be read on the run. It's been written in a way that you could pick it up to read a couple of pages, take on board what you've read and then come back to the book when you're ready.

My writing is based on psychological research that I have conducted or reviewed in the literature. I will refer to it throughout the book; however, have assumed that you are not seeking a textbook. Within each chapter, I have curated additional resources that you may find of interest if you wish to explore certain topics further. In addition, in the back of the book, you will find references to any of the studies that I specifically cite or mention.

The book has been written in a traditional chapter format with headings to help you navigate your way through the book. Each chapter has a short introduction and then within each section one to three pages on any given topic. I have spent many hours sitting through basketball practice, swim squads and touch football training. Small chunks of information make sense to me. Small pieces mean I can spend some time reading and glancing up to watch some of their training. If you have particular priorities, you may wish to head straight there. If so, the below guidelines will help you decide which page to turn to first.

Chapter 1	Because you understand the importance of conversations with your child. You want to gain further insights into how to enhance communication with your child and discover how can you share your messages most effectively, so your child can actually hear you!
Chapter 2	Because you want to understand how your child thinks and help them in their approach to sport. You want them to see the value of the process and not get too hung up on the outcome.
Chapter 3	Because you'd like some strategies in your parenting toolbox to help your teens navigate the tough times. You want them to learn the lessons that will allow them to grow in sport and in life.
Chapter 4	Because you know the mind game is essential. You want to understand better how human psychology works, and you need someone to sift through the mountains of information and tell you what's important.
Chapter 5	Because managing injury can be a minefield. You want your child to be healthy and well, and you need some back up when they are sidelined.
Chapter 6	Because sports are the toy store of life. You want your child to enjoy their sporting experience, and you need strategies for when it gets too serious, or they don't want to play anymore.
Chapter 7	Because this is a substantial commitment for you and your child. You want your child to appreciate their opportunities, and you're curious as to how being grateful enhances performance.
Chapter 8	Because you know you're also a significant part of the puzzle. You want to help your child as best you can, and you want to see what you need to know that helps, while also understanding what doesn't.

Chapter 9	Because you know the relationship your child has with their coach is important. You'd like to know more about how to support that relationship, but also what to do if something is not right.
Chapter 10	Because you know that balance is important. You also know that fitting it all in can be a struggle and you'd like some tips on how to manage sport and enjoy life.
Chapter 11	Because you want to know what the issues are for other parents. You know you face your challenges, and you wonder what other families go through. This chapter shares some of their questions – and my answers!
Chapter 12	The final chapter brings together each of the key concepts of the book, to be sure you got each of the lessons and strategies and are ready to make changes moving forward.

a final word

This book is coming to you from one parent to another. I will share the learnings I have gained through my years working in psychology with families and their children. I will also include, where appropriate my life learnings, which will usually be my mistakes – learn from them rather than replicate them, where you can! Take your time in reading this book, jot down your thoughts and steps moving forward. Revisit chapters from time to time and understand that parenting is always, a work in progress. We do the best we can, learn, and then learn some more! I hope you find it a helpful resource for what we can do as parents as we sit together *in the grandstands.*

IN THE BACKGROUND: HELPFUL CONVERSATIONS

CHAPTER 1

> There's no way to be a perfect parent but a million ways to be a good one.
>
> **Jill Churchill**

PARENTS, FAMILY MEMBERS, COACHES and teachers are critical supports for a teen's sporting life. From your presence in the grandstands to the conversations around the dinner table, when a child's formative sporting years are guided and supported well, it will positively influence their sporting journey.

You can greatly assist a child's development by providing a strong and positive role model and upholding integrity and respect. A sport that is positive, fun and nurturing will have the best outcomes for the teen. However, well-intentioned individuals may, at times, exhibit traits of a 'poor sport' because they lack better guidance and need reliable information. This chapter outlines some of the key factors to consider in best supporting expectations within sport.

discussion points

No matter their age, sport or ability, the discussions you have with your child about their athletic performance need to be positive and free of pressure. How in-depth you go will in part be influenced by their personality, your personality and the developmental stage they are in. For some, it works well to simply ask them how they felt during the session or competition. Other families may choose to have detailed conversations. This is something you and your child will need to navigate and determine together.

Some children like to discuss their training and performances at length, while others prefer not to talk about it at all. A guiding principle is to determine what is helpful for your child. If it helps them to think about the session and to process it by talking to you, then that is something that you want to consider. On the other hand, a child who feels they are being interrogated is less likely to enjoy or see out the conversation!

Car rides can be a great place for conversations. Sitting side by side, eye contact is removed and the power imbalance shifts. Within the car, there are fewer distractions, there's a limit on time, and you have a captive audience! Listening is incredibly important in these conversations. The more you listen, the more opportunity for them to speak. Small prompts, open questions and cues to let them know you are listening will increase the likelihood of a conversation. Please make sure you pick up on the cues if your child does not want to talk and remember to keep your eye on the road!

what do the questions you ask say about you?

The questions you ask your child after competition and games will tell your child what you think is important in sports. If you ask, 'Did you win?' your child will think winning is important. If you ask, 'Did you have fun?' he or she will assume having fun is essential. Your questions are a reflection of your values and tell your child what you consider to be the key priorities. Importantly, your questions will also impact upon your child's motivation.

Consider the following questions and note the values underlying them:

Question	*Values*
How did you go, did you beat Mary?	Outcome and social comparison
Were you pleased with your performance?	Satisfaction
Was that fun?	Fun
Is that your best time?	Personal best
What went better than last time you did that drill?	Improvement
Did you win?	Outcome
What went wrong?	Outcome and process

It's like the universe knows I was writing this chapter! My son and husband have just returned from a basketball game. My 14-year-old son walked in, face as red as a beetroot, beaming smile on his face and our conversation went as follows (with my inside voice in italics):

IN THE BACKGROUND: HELPFUL CONVERSATIONS

Him	'Mum, the score was 48–20.'	
Me:	'Wow, 68 points, that's a lot in one game!'	*I quickly found an observation that wasn't the apparent outcome, plus I was surprised because they often lose!*
Him	'Yes, it was awesome!'	
Me	'And look how red in the face you are! It looks like you must have been working hard.'	*Observation emphasising effort, rather than the outcome.*
Him	'Yes, it was boiling, and we had to do a lot of running.'	
Me	'What did you enjoy about the game?'	*I was expecting us to return to a conversation about the score.*
Him	'Well, the first quarter was only 7–3 and then the second quarter was 14–10.'	
Me	'Sounds like it was an exciting game. Did the turnaround happen in the third quarter?'	*I am still keeping the conversation about the process.*
Him	'Yes, we got four baskets in a row, and they couldn't recover from it. It was like they gave up.'	
Me	'Oh, it's tough when you're on the receiving end of that, isn't it? It sounds like your team got lots of confidence from the momentum.'	*It is emphasising empathy for others – that may well be us next week! It also makes an observation of what his team did well, which will be a helpful memory to draw on in the future.*
Him	'Yes, it was lots of fun.'	
Me	'It sounds like it.'	

I'm not going to pretend that my child doesn't enjoy winning. I don't know too many children that don't. However, it would have been easy to turn the conversation to winning from his opening statement, and my thinking is it would have been a shorter conversation. My point about the outcome versus process is that the process is the aspect that athletes have more control over. Was the team they played today lower, higher or equivalent ability? I'm not sure. A focus on the process today, when there was a win, will make that a typical conversation for us which will be helpful for when they are next on the receiving end of an uneven scoreline. It also told him that I was particularly interested in what happened and how it came about more so than the outcome.

motivating mojo

Motivation is a crucial element to determine effort within sport and explain longevity in staying involved. Motivation falls into two categories: intrinsic and extrinsic. Intrinsic motivators are internally rewarding elements. They are the self-controlling aspects that determine the emotional response to sport. Turning your child's attention to their intrinsic motivators can help them to recognise what keeps them enthusiastic in sport and the reasons why they participate.

In contrast, extrinsic motivators are those elements of influence that occur outside of the individual. These factors can be substantive motivators; however, the level of control an individual has over them may be less than the intrinsic motivators. They are still important, and in fact, understanding the extrinsic motivators can be particularly valuable when motivation wanes.

The following table highlights some examples of the different types of intrinsic and extrinsic motivation.

Intrinsic Motivator	*Extrinsic Motivator*
Attaining a PB	Accountability to someone
Competency	Community
Feels good	Events and competitions
Fun	Friends and teammates
Self-confidence	Praise and encouragement
Self-esteem	Trophies and medals
Wellbeing	Weather

which type of motivation is better?

Both types of motivation have their place. Intrinsic motivation is useful because we can reinforce behaviour from within ourselves, and we are not relying on others. Intrinsic motivation is something you can always rely upon because it is individually determined. Extrinsic motivation, in contrast, is reliant on external factors and is, therefore, potentially more variable and less controllable. This does not mean, however, that it is any less reinforcing. Most athletes have multiple motivators as to why they train and perform. Understanding these motivators is important because when a motivator is removed, a decrease in enthusiasm is likely. Consider that information in the light of this story that has long been told in sport psychology classes.

> An old man returned home one day to find his garden bed trampled. Annoyed, he tended to the plants and repaired them as best he could. The following day, four young teens passed by after school and played a mock game of football on the adjacent block. Occasionally the ball would stray into his yard, and the boys would run through the garden to chase the ball, squashing plants as they ran. The intention of the boys did not seem to be to destroy the garden; instead, they were more excited to retrieve the ball and run it back into play.
>
> The old man came up with a plan. He called the boys over and explained that he was lonely and loved to watch them play from his window. He offered to pay them a sum of money to come and play each afternoon. At first, the boys were delighted and returned with great enthusiasm, eager for their payment. Over time the old man explained that he could not afford to pay as much money and over time reduced the payment. The decrease in cash was mirrored

in the boy's enthusiasm for the task until, eventually, they stopped coming.

What had once been a task undertaken for the pure fun and social enjoyment had shifted to a paid assignment. Once the payment was reduced the motivation for compliance reduced with it.

The moral of this story has since been replicated in laboratory research. Consistently motivation varies according to whether a person is motivated from within or without. Understanding the motivators for participation and effort are essential.

- Athletes who are **intrinsically** motivated will increase that motivation when extrinsic motivators are **added** (for example, athletes who are paid when they achieve a personal best)
- Athletes with strong **extrinsic** motivators will lose enthusiasm when those extrinsic motivations are **reduced** (for example, no longer wanting to go for a walk because the friend you walk with moves away)
- Athletes who consider external rewards as personally valuable may perceive these as intrinsic gains (for example, a scholarship might be viewed as the opportunity to learn and advance, so the chance is chased for personal attainment).

Therefore, the questions you ask as a parent can powerfully impact your child as a reflection of your values and influencer of their motivation. Your child's expectations will develop through their values and motivations. Questions about how they feel, and a sense of competence when in their sport will help them to focus on the important intrinsic motivators. Therefore, be mindful of the questions you ask, as they shape the thinking and motivation of your child.

don't pay to play

Receiving payment as part of the sporting journey is something I have witnessed many times. I will preface this discussion in acknowledging that when I have seen this occur, the intent of the parent or grandparent choosing this strategy has always appeared to come from a good place. It has typically happened when the intention has been to reward or acknowledge effort or (more often) results. Payment has been given as a source to motivate the child to continue down their path and to strive for excellence and high performance.

It doesn't work. Well, that's not entirely true. It doesn't work for long. It will work for as long as the child achieves the targets and receives the payments. These targets might be for scoring goals or attaining a PB. But then the child stops scoring the goals, or their performances take the normal plateaus that we see as children get older, bodies change, and competitors catch up and all of a sudden, the money (and the motivation) stops.

Money or other external rewards take over. You squash the reasons that will keep the child as a lifelong participant in sport. Intrinsic motivation for the fun of it, for the sense of accomplishment, for the opportunity to learn something new gets pushed to the side.

The emphasis on what is important shifts in the child, particularly so when in a team sport. Paying children to play can increase selfish behaviour which works against the fundamental lessons in a team sport. The focus of the payment is often shared with other teammates which can create further challenges for other families.

Paying a child to play in sport damages motivation and increases the likelihood of drop out in years to come. It's not often I set a hard, fast rule for people – I think that people are sensible enough to have the information in front of them and make a personal decision for themselves. This is the one topic where I make an exception. Please don't do it.

Please. Don't. Pay. Children. To. Play. Sport. Ever.

fixed mindset vs. performance mindset

As painful as disappointment can be, those that achieve excellence soon understand that it is not the opposite to success, but rather a crucial part of it. When we experience failure, it is less about what happens to us, and more about how we respond to it that matters. Too often, people walk away at the first sign of failure, when viewing it with an improved mindset could be the difference between long-term disappointment and future success.

Why your mindset matters
Mindset has been extensively explored in psychological research. Professor Carol Dweck from Stanford University has devoted much of her career to understanding the way mindset affects performance. Fundamentally, your mindset is related to your beliefs around whether ability, intelligence and talent are genetically or environmentally determined.

Those with a fixed mindset believe their intelligence is set, and their capacity is not likely to change substantially. A fixed mindset assumes that talent is the most significant predictor of success and can't be changed. The fixed mindset will prevent you from even contemplating working on your unhelpful habits or areas for growth because you are not open to the idea that they can be improved, 'It's just the way I am'. A fixed mindset may result in you giving up prematurely on persevering with a difficult task.

A common conversation I have with coaches is how to help shift the mindset of an athlete. A fixed mindset becomes stressful when encountering change because perseverance is unlikely when we feel helpless in a situation. The self-talk or the excuse of 'it's never going to change' permits us to quit. Similarly, a fixed mindset is problematic for an accomplished athlete. 'I do well because I'm good' has the potential to increase pressure to perform.

In contrast, a growth mindset focuses on achieving improvement through effort, learning and persistence. Extending on the work by Dweck, within sport settings, I refer to this as a *performance mindset*. A performance mindset is a foundation of believing you can improve at anything if you try and are mentally prepared for achievement. When you choose to view the world through a performance mindset, you are more likely to consider your potential rather than be limited by your current ability or circumstances. An athlete with a fixed mindset is motivated to look capable, compared with a performance mindset that is seeking information to help them to learn to be better.

Mindset is one of the single most important factors for predicting performance and outcome for athletes. A performance mindset is what enables you to take disappointment and turn it into a learning experience. Some people think only of talent as the predictor of performance when it comes to sporting prowess, 'she's a natural' as an example – observing someone successful may make it appear as if it comes easily and with minimal hard work or effort. The truth is, that ability limits the highly talented athlete if they don't also apply effort and belief. Reaching the pinnacle of your sport, work, or any other pursuits will only come when you combine talent with effort and a performance mindset.

How can a parent help with their child's mindset?
Mindsets in children are influenced in the way a parent uses language and as a reflection of their actions. Within this, a key form of influence will be how a child is praised or criticised. Praising ability or talent moulds children into a fixed mindset – their success comes from what you are currently noticing about their ability rather than their progress. Ability can be an inconsistent attribute, therefore instilling an unstable platform of confidence in the child. After being praised for success and ability, Dweck found children would not want to risk their 'talented' label and would take safe

and easy tasks rather than the more challenging ones that would extend them and enhance their learning. In a scenario where the children then experienced (set up) repeated failures, their success plummeted further, and when queried about it later, 40% of the group lied about their performance.

To read more on how an athlete can develop their mindset, explore chapter two in my book, *The Elite: Think like an athlete, succeed like a champion.*

IN THE PROCESS: EFFORT OVER OUTCOME

CHAPTER 2

Continuous effort, not strength or intelligence, is the key to unlocking our potential.
Winston Churchill

THE WORLD FEELS VERY outcome driven. We keep score; we measure the bottom line, even ask how your day was expecting a one-word answer. We won, we made a profit, or our day was 'Good', 'Fine' Terrible!'. Whilst we can measure according to the positive or negative, it doesn't tell us too much of the quality of the experience. You may have found this in your conversation with your teens after school. Any question that starts with a 'Did you' or 'How was' is asking for a closed answer that typically results in a yes or no, or a good or bad.

In contrast, an open question is one that invites conversation. 'Tell me about your day' increases the likelihood of a longer conversation.

This chapter will detail some of the practicalities and some of the mindset elements that can be used to enhance conversation and set your child up to open the discussion and reduce some of the pressures around performance.

perfection vs. excellence

It is great when our children hold high standards for themselves. 'Doing well' is a value that can lead to increased effort, striving for success and reaching of potential. People who set high standards are often good at developing goals, maintaining habits and being clear as to what they want to achieve. However, there is a fine line around standards, as a genuine desire to do well can sometimes step into the world of perfectionism.

Perfectionists typically set unrealistic goals for themselves, which results in enormous pressure and all-or-nothing thinking in terms of success or failure, which does not help in the long run. Perfectionism may relate to unrealistic expectations for self, for others, or in the expectations that others hold for you (e.g. coaches or parents).

Have you ever noticed any of the following behaviours in your child?
- Refusing to try anything new or unfamiliar (worried about possible mistakes or risk of failure).
- Being slow to finish a task (because of over-checking to make sure there are no mistakes).
- Procrastination (because it's easier not to start rather than face the possibility of failure).
- Giving up or becoming distressed, angry, irritable or upset if a mistake is made (if they believe that whatever they are working on might be less than perfect).
- The tendency to think in all-or-nothing-terms (if it isn't perfect, it's bad/wrong/stupid).
- A tendency to be unhelpfully self-critical (focusing on perceived weaknesses and ignoring strengths).

Perfection is an impossible target. The perfect athlete? The perfect coach? The perfect parent? No. They don't exist. The challenge with setting a goal of perfection is that it is a recipe for failure and unhappiness.

So, what do you do if your child seeks perfection? I certainly advocate setting goals that will push and extend. Goals that are out of reach, but not out of sight.

The key is to instead strive for **excellence**. I have worked with countless high-performing athletes, teams and coaches. So many of them have been truly excellent at their craft. Not a single person comes to mind, however, who could be placed in the category of perfect. That person or team doesn't exist.

You might argue that some sports lend themselves to perfection. Didn't Nadia Comaneci achieve a perfect 10 in gymnastics in 1976? Yes, she reached seven of them. My experience is that athletes are the harshest critics of all, and even in a sport where a 10/10 score might be attained, most athletes will still be able to find areas that can be improved or could have been better. Interestingly, the Gymnastic Federation have since changed the scoring to remove the possibility of a perfect score.

What about excellence? Well, look no further than the back page of your daily newspaper – article after article of athletes who can be genuinely described as excellent at their craft. Excellence is derived from the Greek word Arete, which describes superlative ability and superiority. It is the notion that a person can reach their full potential. In contrast, perfection was discussed by Aristotle and described as something that had attained its purpose, was complete and was so good that nothing of the kind could be better. That doesn't sound like any person I have ever met.

Excellence is within reach of us. If our goals are considered within the framework of achieving excellence, it is something that can be attained.

So, what conversations can you have with your child when perfectionistic tendencies arise?

Focus on effort rather than the outcome. Your child can control effort far more than the result of an event. Praise your child for working hard over doing well. Invite a conversation about the effort in the performance or practice and how it feels to know they gave their best. If they felt that they didn't, ask what they could do differently next time and wasn't it good to have this session to learn how to be better in the future?

Normalise failure and disappointment. If your child only hears stories of your success, how can they understand that disappointment is a normal part of life and performance? Tell your child about the critical catch you dropped, the team you didn't make, or the time you were worried and scared. Seek out opportunities when others face challenges and disappointments. This is particularly valuable if it is one of their sporting heroes. Children rarely see their sporting heroes as perfect, yet somehow place that expectation on themselves. If you have the opportunity to watch footage of the athlete, do so when they have made a mistake and talk about how they seem to handle it. Recognising that disappointment is not only a normal part of the performance, but a critical component for improving and getting better is a valuable lesson for our children.

Observation of others. Have a conversation with your child about an idol in their sport. It might be Suzy Batkovic, Johnathan Thurston, Michael Jordan, Usain Bolt or Ashleigh Barty. Ask your child if they would describe them as perfect. What was a mistake that athlete made in a crucial moment? The pressure valve can be eased slightly when children realise that the crème de la crème of sport are outstanding athletes, not perfect ones. Excellent is a worthy description of these athletes; perfect is a label none of these athletes would accept.

focusing on personal control

Conversations about the factors that are within/without our power are particularly helpful in approaching sport and life. Understanding the elements, you can control (e.g. effort, time spent practising, your nutrition), versus those you can't (e.g. your opposition, the weather, decisions by the coach or a team member) are helpful in managing our own expectations.

Theoretically, this is such an obvious distinction. Yet the practicalities of focusing on what you can control is a skill where people often experience struggle. The uncontrollable can feel overwhelming: playing in freezing rain, blocking out the criticism by an opposition player, moving on from the significant error you made 20 minutes ago or wanting to get selected in a team and not being chosen. Focus on your own efforts; it's all you can control – certainly straightforward, sensible advice to give, much harder it would seem to follow.

Let me share an analogy that I often use in explaining the importance of controlling the controllable. Imagine I want you to make a delicious sandwich for lunch, and in front of you are a range of potential ingredients. On the counter, you have white bread, a seeded-bread roll, lettuce, tomato, cheese, ham, raw egg, rotten fish, butter, a cup of sugar, pickles, a piece of Lego and a phone charger.

Think now which of the ingredients you might use to make lunch. You might have considered a ham, cheese and tomato sandwich or tomato, pickles, and lettuce on a bread roll. Yum! Think back to when you read the list, and you may have been somewhat surprised to see items that were clearly inedible. Why didn't you include the phone charger in your sandwich? Or why not a rotten fish salad? So now you have a funny look on your face, and you're questioning my sanity!

In this task, it is clear that a piece of Lego or a raw egg won't help with the goal to make lunch. After initially noticing the unusual items you would soon shift your attention to what will help you get the task done, that gets the sandwich made. It is at this point I link the analogy; if the task is to play well, then the elements such as the weather or a comment by an opposition player might be something you would notice, but they are not going to help you reach the final goal. The negative comment from the opposition player is about as helpful as rotten fish!

Distinguishing between the elements you can and can't control is a useful life skill and applying this within sport helps to manage expectations.

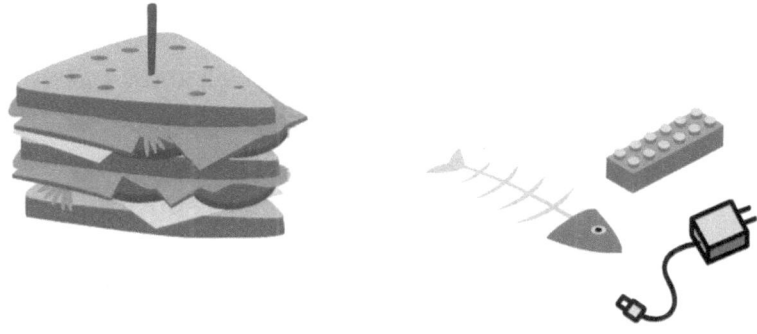

fear of failure

No matter how much we might tell our children that process in sport is more important than winning or losing, we live in a world where often the outcome matters. The sporting headlines in our papers are more focused as to whether your team has won or lost than whether they played well or a particular athlete gave their best. We live in a world where winning is celebrated and, losing is to be avoided.

No wonder then that our children soon learn to set their expectations about the desirability of winning and losing. Children have to live with what can feel like hypocrisy when we tell them that focusing on technique, strategy, effort and process is the aim, yet have them come off the field, court or track and we ask them, 'Did you win?'

With that in mind, a reasonable question to consider is, 'How is performance in sport understood by young athletes?' It was a question that was previously unanswered when I set out to complete my first piece of significant research during my university honours degree. It was the early 1990s, and there was an assumption in the psychological research that winning = success and losing = failure. What I wanted to know is if children viewed this the same way? So, I asked them. I interviewed young athletes aged eight and ten years old, to determine their views on sporting outcomes. For the eight-year-olds, winning was good and losing was bad. The idea that you could win and be disappointed or lose and be happy with the outcome was beyond the comprehension for most I spoke with. This view had shifted by ten years of age. These older children could clearly understand the satisfying loss and unsatisfying win. Indeed, by puberty, we can safely say that teenagers have an understanding of the ambiguity of sport – we can win and not be happy, and we can lose and be pleased with our efforts. What then is happening in the mind of our adolescent athletes when they draw their focus to the outcome?

IN THE PROCESS: EFFORT OVER OUTCOME

Fear of failure is a common experience for athletes. This occurs when the thought of failure becomes debilitating to the point that it affects actions and performance *before the competition has occurred*. I have encountered teen athletes who have chronic diarrhoea in the days before the competition, those who have had sleepless nights worrying about performance, those who have faked illness to avoid playing, and those who become highly irritable in the leading days; all centred around the fear of not being successful during competition. The anticipation and the worry that is anchored to an upcoming performance can have a debilitating or even paralysing effect on a teens ability and willingness to participate.

What can a parent do in this situation? It starts with paying attention to what is happening to your child in the lead up to an event. What have you noticed? What has changed? Is it their actions? Is it in their words? Is it what they are not saying? And now you need to stop and take a breath. What your child does not require you to do is to add together a range of observations, form a conclusion, share it with them only to find out you have completely misread the situation! Let me share an example of this.

> Parent: Janey, you haven't been yourself lately. You've been moody and off your food. When I ask you about training, you seem distracted, and you're getting too concerned about the carnival this weekend. You need to relax more. Otherwise, you're going to work yourself up, and you'll swim badly. It won't go well, and it's because you've talked yourself out of it before it's even begun.

Wow. See what happened there? Lots of observations were made, conclusions were assumed, and then the advice was given all without getting any information from Janey. Let's slow it down and try that again:

Parent:	Janey, I've noticed lately that you haven't seemed yourself. I feel like your mood is different, and you haven't had your usual appetite. Has it felt like that for you?
Janey	Yeah, maybe. I mean, I guess so.
Parent	I wondered if that might be the case. Lots of things can affect how we feel. Have you noticed that anything has been on your mind a lot?
Janey	Nothing specific, I do have a lot going on at school at the moment.
Parent	School can feel like a lot of pressure. Is it more about the schoolwork, or the teachers or outside of the classroom?
Janey	Well, I did get into a stupid argument with …

In this instance, it was nothing to do with swimming. Janey argued with her best friend, and that's what had contributed to the change in behaviours. We also know that teenagers can sometimes know exactly what's going on and other times won't have the insight or won't want to share their inner lives with us. The point I want to share here is more about our reaction. If we are quick to observe, analyse, diagnose and advise, we may be well off the mark. You are going to of course have your theories but remember that we are not with our teens every hour, we don't know what happens throughout their day, and we certainly don't know everything that is happening within their active minds.

What I have found works best is to start with the observation:
⇒ I have noticed …
⇒ It seems to me …
⇒ I don't know how things have been going for you, yet I wonder …

Notice that the language is tentative, interested and open to understanding. Jump in with a conclusion, and even if you are right – it may get rejected.

The common question is, what do you do if they shut you down? An excellent question, and I have been on the receiving end of that professionally and personally! I'll take my earlier example, change Janey's response and show you how I might manage that.

Parent	Janey, I've noticed lately that you haven't seemed yourself. It feels like your mood is different, and you haven't had your usual appetite. Has it felt like that for you?
Janey	Nup, I'm fine (said with a smidge of tone!).
Parent	Ok, I might have misread it then. I just noticed that you hadn't eaten much of your lunch the last few days and you haven't seemed quite your usual self when I've picked you up from school.
Janey	No, I'm fine.
Parent	Ok, well, I want you to know that if you feel like chatting about anything I'm here. I know you've got a lot happening at school and with training, and I understand that it's a lot to manage.

Here I'm no further along in understanding what is happening for Janey – it might be the competition, schoolwork, friendship issues, a social issue in the world that has sparked her interest, something going on with her sibling or an argument with a teacher. Who knows! What I have done is open the door to a conversation down the track.

I would also reassess how the timing of the discussion was and perhaps after dinner, before bed, or even the next morning, if nothing seems to have changed, I might follow up. I would do this by reassuring my availability to chat if that's what she wants or also use non-verbal cues such as an extra-long hug or a hand on her shoulder to communicate connection. Possibly we've all been there when we're feeling out of sorts, and someone repeatedly asks us what is wrong. Patience and saying less but sharing our concern and availability is often the key.

fear of success

If you've read this heading and thought, this must be a typo – I promise, this is real!

There are some teens and adults who feel success is something to be feared or avoided. Let me share with you two case studies of living with a fear of success.

Catherine came to see me as a 28-year-old. Her doctor had referred her for assistance with weight loss. She had been obese for all of her adult years, and her general practitioner had (wisely) identified some psychological background to be addressed. Catherine stated she was keen to lose weight for her health and to feel better within herself but struggled to make the necessary changes. In taking Catherine's history, we discussed aspects of her childhood, her teen years and family background. Catherine was an only child and described the parenting style of her father as being particularly strict. She said she spent her childhood worried about his reaction to her friends, and he told her that she was not to have a boyfriend until she finished school. We explored this further and Catherine recalled the day she realised that if she made herself unattractive to boys, she wouldn't get in trouble from her father. Her relationship with food became the factor that 'protected' her from distress. She stated she feared attractiveness and that was something to be avoided. She expressed she didn't think that fear had ever left her.

Dave came to see me as a 17-year-old with general anxiety. Dave was a successful basketball player within his school, captaining the senior team for the last two years. He had been a representative player since he was 12 years old, and his potential and career progression were assumed within his community and in the local media. His lucky break was imminent. A playing agent had approached his parents, and he had been invited to trial with a state-based open men's team, an unusual opportunity for a player of his age. In the confidence of my office, Dave shared that he was fearful of taking the chance and performing well as then he would move into 'a bigger pond' and have to consistently perform at a level above his current level of comfort. He told me he planned to fake an illness to rule himself out of the trial. The perception he held of success and what that would mean for him moving forward, filled him with anxiety, worry and preoccupation. A fixed mindset resulting in a fear of doing well.

Fear of success is not as common as a fear of failure. I raise it here for two reasons – the first, is to let you know that it is real. Many people struggle to comprehend the worry that might come from being successful. However, for those who experience it, when that worry occupies your thinking, it can be debilitating in terms of performance and future action. It can be the reason that someone places roadblocks in front of themselves and self-sabotages to impact their own possibilities.

The second reason is that if your child articulates a worry about being successful, it is something to respect and discuss, rather than dismiss as ridiculous! Remember that while it might sound silly to others, it is anything but to the person who is experiencing it. In the instance of Catherine, it caused her to self-sabotage her life for 15 years by habit without feeling she had any strategies to overcome it.

The key approach in addressing fear of success is to open up the conversation in a non-judgmental way. Leads you may use could include:

⇒ Tell me what you're thinking …
⇒ I understand you're saying that …
⇒ Doing well can feel like it adds to the pressure …
⇒ What would that mean for you …

If the concerns continue, it can be a useful conversation to have with the coach. You might offer to your child that you could help to facilitate that conversation, or better still help your child determine how they could raise it with their coach.

ability, effort and self-esteem

The relationship between ability, effort and self-esteem is important within children's sport. The honours research I introduced earlier touched on this, but specifically, I was also interested in understanding whether the self-esteem of a child impacted the explanations a child might give when experiencing a win or a loss (e.g. satisfying or disappointing). When we look at the explanations people give to events, they are often explained by one of four key reasons: ability, effort, task difficulty or luck.

An important pattern became evident in the explanations that children gave. Of particular note was that the explanations were strongly influenced according to whether the children had higher or lower self-esteem.

Children who had high self-esteem were those who held themselves in high regard. They had a level of confidence in their performance and felt good about themselves. These were the children that believed success was due to their ability and effort, and failures were due to the task difficulty or bad luck.

Children with low self-esteem were those who held themselves in low regard. They had a poor view of their performance and did not generally feel good about themselves, nor their capability. Their understanding of their success was in complete contrast to the children with high self-esteem. These children believed any success was due to the task being relatively easy, and great luck. Failures were more likely explained by a lack of ability and reduced personal effort.

This has significant value for parents and coaches. Our words are so crucial in reinforcing or challenging the beliefs of our children. To emphasise a child's performance based on their ability shifts the importance to something that they hold relatively little control over. Stop for a moment and think about your ability *right now* in serving in tennis. Perhaps you are great, or maybe you haven't picked up a racquet in 20 years (like me!). Regardless, your ability today, and tomorrow is unlikely to change too much. Expertise in serving takes some time to develop and improve. If I am only encouraged based on my ability, I'm likely to receive few accolades.

Think how different it would be if you encouraged someone based on their effort. Effort is something that can vary in an instant and is predominantly *within your control*. Even if I am a lousy tennis player, I can still try and still be encouraged. Effort is controllable and when I do it, it by itself is reinforcing.

The best way to enhance a child's self-esteem is to reinforce their *effort* rather than their *ability*. This approach encourages a process mindset around performance, puts much less emphasis on the outcome and builds confidence. This focus places control back in the domain of the athlete.

* A note on self-esteem.

I feel the need to apologise to millennials and i-generation. We meant well. In the 1980s and 1990s, the self-esteem movement came along, and our good intentions didn't quite reach the outcome we sought. Let me explain. Psychological research in the 1980s demonstrated a link between self-esteem and success. It became clear that the two variables were related. The further conclusion drawn was enhanced self-esteem should result in better performance and wellbeing.

As a consequence, a significant shift in parenting styles and education resulted in a high emphasis on self-esteem. This is where the well-intentioned plan came unstuck. You can't 'gift' someone self-esteem. If you tell people, they are fantastic, give every child a prize and protect children from the harsh reality of sometimes missing out, all it does is set kids up for long-term pain. A generation has been raised where the majority of children believe themselves to be 'above the average'. There are too many children who have finished primary school having never missed out, never not been picked, and believe that every school assembly is an opportunity to walk across a stage.

It shifted the behaviours of parents too. I was a child of the 70s when parents were portrayed in mainstream media, like the parents from the Charlie Brown Peanuts cartoons. Remember them? No? That's right. They never featured. Childhood with Linus, Lucy, Snoopy and Peppermint Patty explored their friendships and frequent failures. The parents? They were shown as 'text', specifically *Waa, Waa, Waa* from offscreen. Creator, Charles Schulz, said of Charlie that, 'He must be the one who suffers because he is a caricature of the average person. Most of us are much more acquainted with losing than winning'.

The contrast between a typical week for a child of the 1970s versus those in the 2000s is evident. Our modern-day children are heavily scheduled, technologically advanced, better educated, opportunity-filled, and live a completely different life to what occurred two generations earlier. I'm not going to argue which is better or worse, as I've also learnt that it is the job of every age to think their childhood was more demanding than the current generation (I've heard myself tell my sons that very thing!). But what is clear, is that not providing children with enough opportunity to fail (safely) has come at a cost to the current generation. Parents who emphasise effort, hard work and bouncing back rather than overly celebrating success are helping build their childrens' resilience.

IN THE DEPTHS: MANAGING DISAPPOINTMENT

CHAPTER 3

> If you learn from defeat, you probably haven't lost.
> **Zig Ziglar**

LOSING, UNDERPERFORMING, MISSING OUT on selection or making a mistake at an important moment all hurt. Understandably, as parents, we'd prefer to spare our children the pain of disappointment. If only it were that easy! Participating in life means taking risks and making ourselves vulnerable to disappointment.

The life lesson of disappointment is that it is less what happens to us and more how we respond to it that matters. When we can understand that sport provides feedback, and it's how we interpret that feedback that is critical, every disappointment becomes an opportunity to learn and grow.

when it goes pear-shaped

Learning to manage disappointment and to manage personal reactions to distress is an important life skill. It's tough when it occurs, and so as parents, we need to think of this as a skill being taught to our children. Imagine your teen is playing a team sport, the game is close and in the final moments, your child is involved in the play that could win them the game, and they don't. Either because they couldn't convert an opportunity, or they made a mistake that allowed the opposition to win.

Which of the following would you prefer to see as the two teams walk off the field:

a) Your child visibly upset, downcast, stomping their feet and refusing to shake hands with the opposition
b) Your child visibly upset, marching up to you and telling you how bad the referees were, how rough the opposition played, and how it isn't fair
c) Your child visibly upset, shaking hands with the opposition, coming off the field talking with their teammates.

Clearly, a set-up for answer 'c' by me! What I'd like you to note is that in all instances, I acknowledge that the child is in some way visibly upset. That's ok. We know that when something happens, that disappoints us, it may be evident to others. Particularly when it is children, it can be challenging to mask. I'd also note that there may well have been poor decisions by the officials, and opposition teams might be rough. What doesn't help our child is for us to reinforce poor sporting behaviour.

The expectations I would recommend for parents in this instance is that conversations about coaching decisions, calls by referees, whether your child was thrown a bad pass by a teammate or other complaints that are unfair … are car trip conversations. Children need to learn that playing sport is a gift, and that to walk off the court, field, arena or any other terrain with their opening lines as a complaint, lacks gratitude and grace.

Importantly the message to the child is not that those topics are not open for conversation, but they are best had with the benefit of a small passage of time. Allow them to finish their sport, grab a drink, have a shower, and then the conversation is likely to naturally temper down a little.

Of course, managing strong emotions in our children is a challenge for parents, and we do this best when we are regulating our own feelings. You may agree with your child and what has them upset. Regardless, calming down and having a conversation rather than buying into a hot pot of angst is a much better way to manage what happened. We would never recommend to anyone to handle a work situation while highly charged with emotion, so it follows we would encourage our children in the sports arena to regulate their emotions appropriately.

Managing disappointment is frequently witnessed on post-event sports interviews and commentary at the elite level. Teenagers often like to watch the reactions of the stars, and this can be a helpful conversation starter.

Within the National Rugby League, North Queensland Prop Josh McGuire demonstrated the power of doing this well after his team's disappointing loss (the team had only won 3–9 for the season). With a myriad of possible excuses at his disposal, McGuire chose to say, 'We've all got to put our hands up and get back to work, it's not good enough at the moment'. McGuire's quote was followed up by subsequent outstanding personal games for his team, showing great determination and effort. He took personal responsibility and then he walked his talk.

Our sporting stars offer opportunities for dinner time conversation, take those opportunities and have those discussions where you can. There is much to be learned from life's disappointments.

normalising grief

Whenever people experience a loss or a disappointment that is unwelcome or upsetting, we commonly respond with a reaction that is likened to grief. While the loss of a soccer match is clearly different to the loss of a loved one, there are some consistent features in our responses – and recognising these can help to make sense of our reactions to it.

The grief response was first explained by Swiss psychiatrist Elizabeth Kübler-Ross, encompassing five stages:

- Denial – a time of disbelief. The situation doesn't feel real; we can feel numb or as if it's all part of a horrible dream.
- Anger – when we are fearful or worried, we often express our emotions through anger. We may be short-tempered or feel angry.
- Bargaining – in need to regain control, it is common to ask, 'what if' and 'if only' questions. We try to negotiate alternative options to numb the grief experience.
- Depression – feeling sad or overwhelmed by our circumstances. This time can feel quiet and helpless.
- Acceptance – while we don't have to like a situation, we need to accept it has happened before we can move on. Our acceptance lies in understanding our circumstances.

In explaining grief, Kubler-Ross did not intend to present five distinct stages of a process that someone moves through from beginning to end. If only life were that simple! However, this is often how it is viewed. My experience in supporting those who grieve is that the response is anything but a series of ordered steps. At any moment, we may jump between or combine the five stages, and it can be messy. In a visual sense, their combination is better likened to a bowl of spaghetti than ordered steps.

When facing disappointment, your child's subsequent reaction is likely to be both unpleasant and normal. The strategies below can provide comfort and guidance to help you encourage them to move forward:

1. **Pay attention and notice the emotions they are feeling.** All feelings are functional. They give us feedback on how we are feeling, so that information is helpful.
2. **Know that our actions are related to how we feel.** If we spend too long grieving for what is lost, we lose the opportunity to move forward to the next possibility. The way we think defines our emotions, so be mindful of negative self-talk.
3. **Ask the question: What is helpful now?** Is there a different way to think or something different that your teen can do? Can you help switch the focus to something that is more positively reframed?
4. **Get creative.** Setbacks can often lead to opportunity. Is there new learning you can help your child adopt? What can they do now, so that they might one day look back and see this time as a blessing?
5. **Be patient.** There is no set timeframe for the grief response and sometimes we simply need to ride it out.

It is important to keep disappointment in perspective. Missing out on a representative team, not getting picked for the Olympics or losing a grand final is certainly disappointing, and it is legitimate to be upset by the result. The intensity of the grief response will vary as it is an individualised reaction. I personally remind myself through disappointments that whilst a 'bump in the road', if it hasn't featured in the first three stories of the six o'clock news, then it could have been worse!

why losing is good for you

The challenge with frustration is, that it undermines clarity of thinking. Frustration usually develops when behaviours and actions are not in keeping with expectations, and we become annoyed and irritated. There may also be a level of underlying fear that further exacerbates frustration. The ability to process, work through and helpfully reshape thinking becomes critical in managing disappointment. Ultimately it all comes down to self-dialogue, awareness and effective action.

Given this is a life skill most adults are still to master, it should not be a surprise when in a moment of high adrenaline, a teenager is not appropriately equipped to well manage a reaction. Turning to the child in the immediacy of the disappointment and offering, 'You know losing is good for you?' is most likely flint for an argument. Regardless, there are lessons to be gained from losing, and it would be a wasted opportunity to not learn it (at some later stage). The other observation I would make is that failing to pay attention to the lesson will only mean that life will find another way to teach us again!

The timing here is crucial. Finding a time to notice when something hasn't gone to plan and understand why that might be the case is important. My youngest once took it upon himself to build a table for his bedroom and spent each afternoon for two weeks using every tool in our house to create the table. The finished product was a bit shaky and he had put a brace on back to front, regardless he thought it was great – and so did we. The moment of truth arrived to place it in his bedroom. It was a large table. Sadly, it didn't fit down the corridor to his room! He then spent another day pulling it apart and rebuilding it inside his room. What an opportunity for learning a lesson! I am hoping he's learnt about measurement and planning from the experience. The other lesson for us is that if we ever sell our home, we may well be selling it with a table!

Sport is the same. When your child arrives at their game without their boots – let them learn the lesson. In future, they will check their gear every time they leave the house. If your child understands that she gets disqualified in breaststroke each time she doesn't place both hands on the wall on the turn, she'll soon learn to start putting them there.

Disappointment is a valued teacher. Don't miss the lesson and where you can, allow your child to learn it. Appropriately timed you might say something like, 'I can see you're disappointed about today's game/race/practice. Sometimes, the best thing to come out of something that didn't go the way we planned is to learn how to make it better next time. What is something helpful to take out of today?'

learning from success

Success leaves clues.

Most elite teams will have a regular team meeting following competition. One season with a particular team, I recorded the duration of those meetings. Interestingly, and possibly not surprisingly, the team meetings following a loss were more than twice the length of the meetings following a win. Upon discussion with the coach, we considered the importance of prioritising the elements that had led to the victory, as equally, if not more important than the losses. As an intervention, the coach agreed to lengthen the meetings with the team following a win. This allowed the team to consider in greater depth their successful actions.

Experiencing a win, or success is too often brushed off with relief. Athletes will benefit when they pay attention to what they're doing well. Is your child able to tell you what they enjoyed about the event? They may well tell you winning, and fair enough! If you can, shift their focus to what it was about the competition itself that they enjoyed. What did they do that allowed them to compete or train well? What aspect made them feel capable and competent? It doesn't need to be any more than a conversation in the car heading home. The key benefit is them hearing themselves say out loud what they did well.

Helpfully, you can then draw back on this conversation in the future. For example, if your child isn't performing well or they express worry about an upcoming performance, then drawing on the actions of their success can be helpful.

Success leaves clues so pay attention to them.

process over outcome

Of all the messages coaches repeat across sports, and levels of expertise, it is the value of process over outcome. From the junior ranks of the sport, encouraging an athlete to pay attention to the task at hand, and the process itself rather than what happens at the end of the competition is key. 'Pay attention to what you are doing, the scoreboard will take care of itself,' is one of the most important, and one of the most challenging mental skills for athletes to conquer.

Within elite sport, there is no doubt than many athletes set goals relating to winning, achieving personal best or where they may place in an event. The challenge is to understand that it is the micro-skills within the sport that will enhance their likelihood of achieving that goal. No Olympic swimmer has achieved gold by only focusing on that medal in the lead-up to an event. Much more likely, their thinking has been centred around race plan, technique, strategy, pacing, breathing and self-talk.

A further advantage of focusing on process in the lead-up to the competition is that it serves as a strategy to reduce anxiety. If your teen is approaching an event and finds themselves getting agitated on whether they will place in the top five in the cross country (to progress to the next level in your region), this shift in focus can work beautifully to refocus them.

'What does it take to run and finish well?' could be the question. Their answer might be about pacing, attacking the hill with confidence, keeping the body relaxed and a focus on breathing. While the attention shifts to those specific skills, it moves the focus away from the outcome (the most uncontrollable element).

A common mantra by coaches is to 'trust the process' and then an athlete can perform at their best. Whenever we put our trust into something we inwardly smile and relax – both elements that are conducive to our highest performance.

the curse of the PB

Striving for your personal best (PB). It is an emphasis often made by coaches, and with good reason. It shifts the athlete's attention to their performance and away from their competitors. I can recall the surprise when I first heard a (swim) coach say that they wished kids didn't set goals to achieve PBs. At first, it didn't make sense to me – why would setting your personal best not be an aspiration? However, when typical patterns of skill acquisition and personal best for junior and beginning athletes is considered, the reason to be careful with PBs became evident.

It is generally the case that with practice, performance improves, particularly when learning a new skill or within the body of the growing athlete. Imagine the swimmer who participates in swim squad from an early age and competes at carnivals between the ages of eight and twelve years. These athletes often have an exponential improvement in their swim-times. These gains are usually a combination of:

- hours spent training. Hours of practice in the pool is typically high for swimmers
- competition being a few weeks apart (so performance is measured regularly)
- healthy growth through these formative years.

It is not unusual for swimmers to consistently attain PBs for years at a time as younger athletes. This offers a great sense of achievement and is understandable, given the work and effort, and maturational growth. The downside of consistently achieving a PB is that it can quickly become an expected outcome. Again, not a problem until the developmental plateau occurs.

As athletes refine their expertise, and physically mature, it becomes difficult and eventually impossible to improve every time

IN THE DEPTHS: MANAGING DISAPPOINTMENT

they compete. A plateau in performance will commonly occur. Elite athletes come to understand that this is the stage where the body maintains while the athlete needs to work harder or refine their technique further for small improvement.

From a physiological and coaching perspective, this makes perfect sense. For the athlete going through it, it can be a frustrating and perhaps even de-motivating time. For an elite athlete, the plateaus can be lengthy, and a personal best may not be achieved for months, even years at a time. The novice will continue to have far more significant improvements while the elite performer may feel they are battling for just a fraction of gain.

I have already highlighted the motivational dangers in paying children in the sports arena. Therefore, you can imagine the damage this can do when payment is tied to personal best performances.

I have witnessed families in individual sports reward their children by keeping tally of their PB performances throughout their season and then depositing a lump sum in their bank account. This is a guaranteed way to shift motivation from the true focus on personal best in an unhelpful way. As one parent once told me, 'It saves them getting a part-time job'.

I'm just going to leave that there.

when your child says, 'no more'.

'I've had enough, I don't want to train/play anymore.' Retirement. This can be a tough time for athletes and their families, particularly if they are 14 years old! The reasons for wanting to stop are varied. The most common reason cited by children is when they feel sport is no longer fun. Around 70% of children will stop playing organised sport by 13 years of age and lack of fun is the number one reason.

There is merit in a conversation with your child when they declare they no longer want to play, so you can understand their reasoning behind it. What is going on behind the decision? Are they worried about their performance? Are they concerned about disappointing you? Is there a personality clash with another player? Is there a conflict with the coach? Is your child being bullied?

The act of listening to your child here is critical. There are not many activities in a child's life where they can have control of the decision making. Sport is the fun, optional extra that children get to do. It's their body, so it is ok to let this be a decision about their time and energy.

The timing of the announcement, and subsequent decision is significant. A child saying before a new season that they don't want to play is quite different from a child saying mid-season or a few weeks in that they want to finish up. Opinions around this can vary. I know many parents (and include myself here) who value the importance of finishing a commitment, particularly when there are teammates who will be affected – or if you have just paid the registration fees and bought new shoes and uniforms! The message in our household has always been that if you start a season, then you finish a season.

If your child is insistent then I would consider a conversation around, well let's go for another two weeks and see how you feel after that.

Parents can worry about what quitting might teach your child in terms of perseverance, and so, the best decision for your child

IN THE DEPTHS: MANAGING DISAPPOINTMENT

will have several considerations. Understanding your child's passion for the sport is important. Just because they are good at the sport doesn't mean they will always have a passion for it. If your thinking starts to gravitate to, 'I would have given anything to have your talent' then hear the warning bells. This is about your child, not you.

It is important to be mindful of your reaction within this scenario. When I hear a parent say, 'I've invested so much money in [insert sport here]' I am concerned. Re-read those words, 'I've invested'. Most likely a few years in any sport means the money spent has been sizeable, I would guess probably in the thousands. That is a fact: children's sport is expensive.

Comparatively, your financial investment is $0. You have not invested a cent in your child's sport. In the economic sense, an investment is an expense with the intention in the future to create wealth. Your child is not a commodity, and the majority of athletes will return no money for playing their sport. You have unquestionably spent money; I would imagine lots of it. I know that by the time I pay registration, game fees, have bought uniforms, boots, equipment, fuel costs to drive to training sessions and games – the cost is considerable. It is, however, not an investment.

To speak of any extracurricular activity as an investment is problematic in terms of how you consequently view it. It is an expense, and if you allow your child to participate with no expectations of financial return or performance outcome, it will help to reduce some of the pressure that you will subtly be placing upon them.

It's important to respect the wishes of a child to make a decision, even if you think they may regret it with time. Sometimes that is the important lesson. My youngest once dug his very capable heels in when he decided he no longer wanted to swim. I persevered with him participating to the end of the season, and then he was firm that he was never going back. Ever. Last year, some three years, later he announced that I should never have let him quit! After laughing hysterically (in front of him), I reminded him about the consequences of our decisions, and that it wasn't too late for him to head back to the pool! I may have also pointed out the important life lesson that his mother is often right!

IN THE MIND: MENTAL STRATEGIES

CHAPTER 4

Failure isn't fatal, and success isn't final.
Winston Churchill

THE JOB DESCRIPTION OF parent is extensive! Taxi driver, concierge, chef, hairdresser, laundromat, protector, disciplinarian, doctor and deliverer of hugs and love. Whilst it can feel like we need to tick every box, the reality is we won't and we can't. Regardless, it may be helpful to understand some of the science behind sport performance, particularly sport psychology.

The way you think matters. An athlete's mental preparation is a key predictor for performance. Understanding some of the elements and application of sport psychology can be useful as we and our children travel through that journey.

speaking the lingo

Sport psychology is a science aiming to understand people in sport. It can also be a wordy, lofty discipline that takes simple concepts and overly complicates them! It is the very human nature of its focus, that at times becomes its most significant criticism. How do you measure those parts of being human that sit deep within our heads? There are times when, as researchers, we can't even agree as to what we are measuring!

Take motivation as an example. Looking back through the lecture notes I deliver to the students at university, I have them consider motivation as:

- An *internal personality* characteristic, 'She was highly motivated throughout her career.'
- An *external* influence, 'I want to win it for the people who have supported me and my region.'
- A *consequence* of an *explanation*, 'I didn't perform as well as I intended because I just didn't feel motivated on the day.'

This is important to consider as there are many terms within sports psychology which are frequently used, yet with different understandings: grit, mental toughness, confidence, motivation, persistence and effort as a few examples. Some of these concepts have been tossed around for years without resolution as to their meaning.

When I am speaking with a coach, and they tell me that an athlete needs more 'mental toughness', regardless of what a range of textbooks state, what I need to do is find out what that coach means by the term. When it comes to those conversations, it is the coach's definition that I need to understand, not what is in the textbooks. The same applies for you when talking to your teen.

your role in the mental game

This next section will help to clarify some of the specific skills taught within the field of sport psychology. Before we get to that, let's consider your role. You do not need to add to everything you are already doing, a qualification in sport psychology. Nor is it on your shoulders to resolve all these issues for your teen. It is more helpful for them in many cases if you don't fix them, but rather be there to support them along the way.

Please remember that as a parent to your child, your key role in their sporting journey is to support them, rather than to take the role of coach or psychologist (unless you are the coach!). Your child needs 'a soft place to land', and you providing this support will help them greatly in striving for their goals. If they know they have someone to talk to without feeling the pressure that the conversation is going to end as a lecture it will increase the desire of your child to speak to you. This approach most likely will strengthen your relationship with them further.

My reason for including the skills of sport psychology is to broaden your knowledge around what is involved, as it may help you in some of the conversations with your teen. Think of it as background information for you. It may also be that there are some techniques here that you might like to put in place for yourself. Life is a constant lesson and I always consider myself as, 'a work in progress'. There are plenty of sport psychology strategies that will work in other life domains and at any age!

Parents have a significant role to play in helping their child navigate through life, and sport provides a specific context where life conversations can take place. The advantage of knowing something about these sport psychology techniques is it might help in discussions with your teen. For example, if they are talking about trouble getting to sleep at night because they are thinking about the upcoming game on the weekend you might then be able to ask them if they have tried the breathing strategies they have learnt. Please don't feel the responsibility to become the mental skills coach, just know there are strategies there to help your teen and here is some information for you to understand them better.

Within sport psychology, we use a range of mental strategies to assist athletes in regulating their thinking, managing the challenges of their sport, enhancing their learning of skills and techniques, and to maximise athletic performance. These are strategies that might be integrated within your teen's training sessions or skills they may be taught explicitly by a sport psychologist or other mental skills coach. There is, however, nothing to stop you from trying some of the techniques for yourself to improve your performance. There is no better way to understand than to learn for yourself!

Options for learning sport psychology skills with online activities can be explored at https://www.drjolukins.com/in-the-grandstands

IN THE MIND: MENTAL STRATEGIES

how can you cross the language divide?

The key here is to *seek understanding*. If a teen said, 'I'm not feeling motivated to go to training' I would suggest that statement needs to be unpacked further to understand what they mean. As an example, let's have a look at how the conversation could go:

Teen	I'm not feeling motivated to go to training tomorrow.
Me	Tell me some more about not feeling motivated, what's happening for you?
Teen	My body just feels exhausted, and I can't be bothered to go.
Me	It sounds like you're feeling tired and a bit flat?
Teen	Yep.
Me	If you were feeling more motivated, what would be happening for you? What would be different?
Teen	Well it wouldn't be so hard to get out of bed for training.
Me	You usually get out of bed without a problem, so has something changed?
Teen	Yes, well it's gotten colder, and when the alarm goes off, I just don't want to move in my bed and get cold. Walking to the bathroom is the worst, the floor is so cold. I hate the thought of it.

Can you see where the conversation has now shifted? It's actually about how warm the bed is and how cold the floor is in the morning! I would suggest it's less about motivation and more about comfort. The thought of getting up on a cold morning is now the focus, and the teen is attributing that to their lack of motivation. Most people I know would rather stay in bed on a cold morning!

This conversation could then move to strategies to increase comfort (like wear warm socks or slippers) and also have warm clothes ready to change into so the task of getting up isn't quite so unpleasant. It might even mean the lure of a hot chocolate after training to make the early start more bearable.

The teen has referred to motivation, but in fact, it is something else. The importance of the conversation between you and your teen is always to understand the meanings they have for the terms they use. One of the best ways to determine this is to open the conversation, show interest and try to understand from their perspective.

IN THE MIND: MENTAL STRATEGIES

the goldilocks principle

Athletes are more likely to perform at their best when they have the optimal blend of energy and calm focus. It's a delicate balance that can be challenging to achieve. Quite quickly, an athlete can 'tip-over' from being keen and ready, to tense and anxious in the seeming blink of an eye. The sight of a competitor, an unhelpful comment, or focusing too much on winning or losing and an athlete becomes over-aroused and likely to underperform. The relationship between performance and mental readiness has been best described by the inverted-u curve (otherwise known as the Yerkes-Dodson Law).

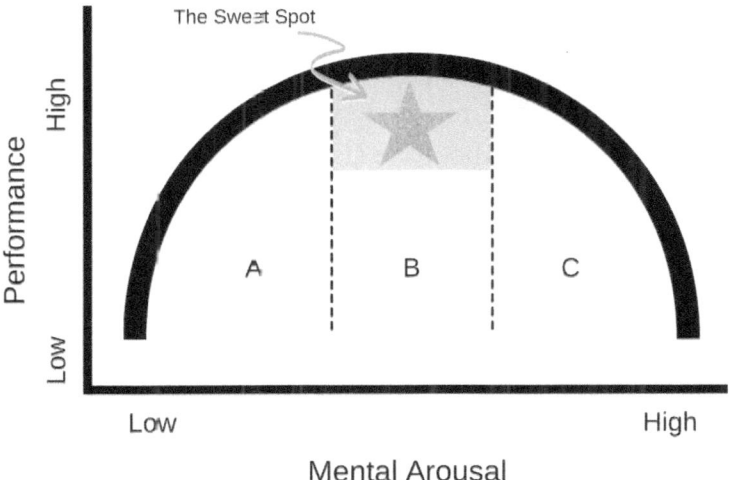

In Zone A of the image, an athlete has low mental arousal. They may report feeling 'flat', tired, or like the event is over. It's the equivalent feeling to running a 100m final 30 seconds after getting out of bed in the morning.

In Zone C of the image, an athlete has high mental arousal. Their mind is spinning, their heart is racing, or their stomach is doing backflips. It's the equivalent to concentrating on the match-winning putt in golf while finding out you've just won gold lotto!

In Zone B of the image, the athlete is in the mental sweet spot. What I sometimes like to refer to as the Goldilocks Zone. Their mental focus is not too low, not too high, but just right.

The ability to keep yourself within the optimal performance zone requires the balance between tension and relaxation, the right focus for the moment and being mentally aroused to perform without overthinking the task. This can be a tough ask of anyone, particularly when you are a teenager new to building your mental skills.

Keeping yourself in the optimal performance zone may require subtle changes (physical or psychological). I recommend the following steps:

> Pay attention to where you are in relation to the curve. Do you notice yourself feeling flat (A), ready to go (B) or agitated/pumped up (C)?
> - ⇒ If A, you may need to increase your mental arousal – think about the task at hand, review your goals or get up and move around, go for a light jog or do some stretches.
> - ⇒ If B, continue to check in with yourself now and again and keep yourself in this zone, ready to compete or train.
> - ⇒ If C, inhale/exhale. It's not possible to be tense and relaxed at the same time. Breathing can help you to focus and calm yourself. Remind yourself at this moment you are fine. Visualise what you can control.

Knowing where an athlete is mentally is best gauged by the athlete. We may be able to observe behaviours that suggest tension or relaxation, but only the person themselves will know what they are thinking and feeling.

mental commentary

Our brain is amazing. It keeps us alive, regulates our sleep cycle, controls our balance, understands language and controls our breathing as just some of its essential functions. Besides, it provides us with our internal commentary on the world – for every moment we are awake! From the moment the alarm sounds in the morning, to the peace of drifting off to sleep at night, we are analysing, evaluating, judging, and observing the outside world and our actions in it.

In a nutshell, the way you think matters. The way you think is intricately linked to how you feel, and it is our feelings that drive the majority of our behaviours.

Humans are also prone to what is known as the negativity bias. A propensity to take a situation and assume the worst. When two things are being considered, perhaps even of equal intensity, the element you will be most drawn to, notice most, pay more attention to, will be the negative.

As humans, we are more likely to:
- remember negative experiences better than positive ones
- recall insults better than praise and compliments
- react more strongly to negative feedback
- think and worry about negative things more frequently than positive ones
- respond more strongly to negative events than to equally positive ones.

Any wonder that sometimes our teen athletes hang on to the negative, ruminate and worry about what has gone wrong, or struggle to see the good. It's the most natural path for our brains to take, and when it forms as a habit, we repeat it without even realising that we are doing it.

Examples of negative bias in sport
- An athlete receives feedback from the coach on their game, which was quite positive overall and noted strong performance and achievements were made. A few constructive comments pointed out areas where improvement could be made, and the athlete fixates on those remarks. Rather than feeling good about the positive aspects of the feedback, they feel upset and angry about the few critical comments.
- An athlete still vividly recalls making an error in a critical moment of a team sport, even though the game happened years ago. They still feel huge regret and find themselves cringing with embarrassment over it, even though no-one else in the team probably remembers it.

self-efficacy

At the essence of sport psychology is the understanding that when we hold on to our thoughts, they soon become our truth. Those thoughts then appear through our actions, and over time they become consistent habits. Ultimately what started as a thought becomes our successes and failures. Henry Ford is credited with the famous quote, 'Whether you think you can or think you can't, you're right!' Well worthy of its place on motivational stickers the message reminds us of the importance of our thoughts in relation to our outcomes.

Self-efficacy is the term used to describe our level of self-belief relative to our capabilities. When our self-efficacy is high, we believe we are well able to do a task (for example, completing a layup in basketball); when our self-efficacy is low we think we're not able to complete a task with competency (for example, my forehand in tennis is not great).

Self-efficacy is important because our intention to attempt a task is influenced by our belief that we can do it. People indeed take on new tasks frequently yet may shy away from something they have tried before without success or believe the likelihood of success is low.

I once worked with a footballer who would catch a high ball as part of his role in the team. It was his job, he was known for it, the team counted on it. One day he made an error, he dropped the ball. The day wasn't any day, it was the grand final, and the error soon followed by his team conceding points. Unfortunately, they lost the game. A new permanent belief was created in an instant. He went from being capable to hopeless in a split second. Even though he had years of evidence to say he could do it, that one moment was significant enough for him that he not only questioned his ability to do that task but did not put himself in a position to do so for the following three years.

Self-efficacy, whether we hold the belief accurately or not, is a strong influencer to our performance and success.

Importantly, self-efficacy is not necessarily directly correlated with our confidence. In the example of the footballer above, it was. The way he thought, the belief of his competence and his resulting self-esteem were all tied into the one experience. Something that the whole team could rely upon him for, fell apart in the moment where it was needed. Rather than forgiving himself for being human, understanding the pressure of the moment, he assumed he was useless, awful, incompetent and a failure – and that is where his view stayed for a long time. He defined himself in a single moment, and his assessment was brutal.

My forehand in tennis, is quite awful. That being said, I have no aspirations for myself as a tennis player (as much as I love watching the game), and so, therefore, I am resilient to my low ability. I am genuinely a below-par tennis player, and I am a robust human despite that. None of my overall self-worth is anchored to my ability to play tennis.

A parent recently asked me, 'My son is so critical of himself. It makes no sense as he has so much potential and ability, but so much doubt. How do I help my child to understand how good he is?' Isn't it tough when you can see how hard your child works, their potential and then those times when they don't choose to see it? This is tricky terrain, because we know, that when we doubt ourselves, someone else telling us of our capabilities doesn't always resonate. We think they are being kind, or they don't really know what we're like. Mental self-sabotage is real across the lifespan.

I do talk to athletes about the importance of spending time recognising what they do well. Through the negativity bias, we too often pay more attention to our failings, give them more weight, and allow it to consume more of our thinking. Successful teams and athletes need to notice what they do well ... because that is what they need to repeat to keep success moving forward. Agonising only over your defeats will never allow you to repeat the elements that make up success.

A simple strategy is to keep a diary of 'yay' moments. A whole training session or competition doesn't need to be amazing, but it's important to notice the small things that went well. Record those moments in a notebook, with the date and the event.

> For example:
> Monday 6th July – Gym session
> Completed core session well; good form through bench press.

Noticing the things that go well provides a diary of success. The successes don't guarantee the belief but can serve as evidence. The activity shifts the thinking of the athlete from a negative to a positive focus, which is also helpful.

Belief has to be generated from within. You can't supply someone with confidence, but you can provide an environment where it's ok to speak (with humility) about achievements. I am unapologetically clear with athletes that success is about knowing (within yourself) what you do well. Focusing on your accomplishments reinforces why you participate in sport.

This is one of those areas, where as a parent, you have to be the safe place for conversation. Where your children can say out loud where they see their strengths and their limitations and can work their way through how they understand their abilities, capabilities, efforts and strengths.

goal setting

Crucial to high performance, goal setting can be focused on performance or process.

Performance focused goals are centred around the outcome for the athlete and are likely to involve achieving a personal best or placing within an event. For example, a long jumper performing 3cm further than their best jump or placing second in a competition.

Process focused goals shift the attention of the athlete to the task at hand and in addressing the 'how' of performance. A process focus considers the technical elements necessary for success. For example, the basketballer who is taking a layup might focus on the process of attack the hoop, secure the angle, eyes up, lock the target, read the defence, controlled footwork, protect the ball, ball release, follow through.

Which is better? Well, both have their place. It is unrealistic to say to any athlete to not focus on the outcome or the performance of their endeavours. However, if it is their sole focus, it won't be performance-enhancing in the long run. Only setting performance goals means that you end up on the start line with a heart full of wishful thinking. Wanting to win or do your best is not going to help you set the plan that will get you there. There's nothing wrong with wanting to win or achieve a PB, but it is something to spend less time thinking about compared to what will get you there.

Process goals can be incredibly helpful because they assist an athlete to define the pathway to the end point. I think of performance goals as the final destination and the process goals as the road to success. The beauty of process goals is, they become the focus if an athlete is expressing concern about an upcoming performance.

Teen	I feel worried about today's game.
Parent	What is worrying you?
Teen	What if I don't go well, what if I lose?
Parent	It's easy to think about when it's over, but let's get you there first. Let's think about what you will control. What do you want to be able to do today, what will competing well look like for you?
Teen	Well, I will be calm and focused, my technique will be good and so will my pace.

The beauty of that conversation is that it shifts the focus from the worry of the outcome to the practicality of the process. You have far less control over the outcome and far more influence over what you do in the performance. Whenever you can, emphasise the value of the process over the outcome.

SMART goals

If you don't know where you are going, how will you know how when you get there?

Goals are a crucial strategy in setting our path and achieving what is important to us. With that in mind, I have found time and time again that athletes, at times, struggle to set goals which will work for them. They have an idea as to what they are working towards, but by not setting them in the best possible way, they limit their chances of success.

The starting point for goals is, to begin with, what success will look like. It's about knowing where you are and where you want to be. You are starting at A and finishing at Z – you need to be able to say what Z will look like! Is it about being faster, stronger, more accurate, winning something or being selected in a team? And yes, that is an outcome goal. Once your Z can be clearly defined, then the process can be determined following five key criteria.

Fortunately, it's easy to remember: we want to set SMART goals.

S	Specific	What exactly do you want to achieve? What will it look like when it's happened?
M	Measurable	How will you measure the goal? Will there be a visible outcome? Can you measure its quality or quantity?
A	Attainable	Is it something that you can achieve? Do you have the resources you need to attain it? The goal aims to be out of reach, not out of sight.

R	Realistic	Is this a suitable goal in your life right now? While it might be attainable, what is the cost in setting out to achieve it?
T	Time-based	When is it going to happen? This week? This month? This year?

This is a model that many coaches use with their athletes, and a conversation around setting goals might look like this:

Athlete	I want to get a PB and qualify for nationals this season.
Coach	Great. What are we aiming for? 200m, 400m, 1500m? {note: Specific}
Athlete	Well, 400m is what I want to focus on.
Coach:	Well your 400m is sitting at 4:15:02. We're looking at the 0.85 sec improvement to qualify for nationals, which is possible in the timeframe, it's going to take some solid work between now and then. {note: Measurable}
Athlete	That sounds good. I'm up for it. I can get 0.85 no worries.
Coach	I'm glad you're keen, but we have to make this attainable. We need to see where we can find the time. (Part of this conversation includes where the focus should be to improve. They jointly agreed his pacing through his turns was a weakness that needed addressing.) {note: Attainable}

Athlete	Ok, so I need to do extra work on my turns. The school production has finished now, so I've got some extra time to stay back at practice to work on that and work on my core some more at the gym, which I haven't been doing. {note: Realistic}
Coach	Good. So now we need to work through the racing schedule and plan out where you should see the benefits of that work, and where we're going to hold back because the training load will be high. {note: Time-based}

Successful goals are clear to what is going to be achieved (specific), identify what success will look like (measurable), are within reach of the athlete (attainable) doable within their commitments and pick a point in the calendar where they are to occur (time-based).

SMART goals are the go-to principles used within sports coaching. I do add an extra letter to the end of the acronym and, that is an E for Evaluate. Goals are no use in the bottom of a drawer. A commitment is necessary to evaluate the goals, determining their progress, and if needed, tweak them a little. None of that can happen if a goal isn't evaluated.

Understand I am not suggesting you set your child's goals. Goals are best set with the coach. However, it may well be that your teen talks to you about their goals, and it is helpful for you to have this background knowledge. You may also like to set your own personal goals and the SMARTE approach can help you.

habit formation

One of the excellent life skills taught through sport is the opportunity to develop self-regulation, discipline and helpful habits. Whether it be holding back when a referee's call goes against you, congratulating the opposition when you lose or going to bed early because you have to get up early the next morning for training, sport serves as an academy for great choices.

This is important, because as adults, we know that making better choices isn't always the natural action. With humans making around 30,000–40,000 decisions every day, is it any wonder we finish the day and the week tired and ready to take the easy options? The more of our everyday that can include helpful habits, the better placed we are to achieve our goals.

We are not always motivated ... so we need to learn discipline.

We will not always be disciplined ... so we need to develop habits.

Willpower is a resource that we often tell ourselves is limited, that once we have exhausted our supply for the day, then we are much more vulnerable to unhelpful habits.

As parents, we help our teens to learn and form their habits. We do this through what we teach and reinforce for them, and from what we demonstrate for ourselves. I'd like to share with you, what I refer to in workshops as 'The Secret Bullet' for goal setting and habit formation. This can be gold in getting our children to modify their behaviour.

Humans live much of their lives following contingencies. That is, our behaviour follows sequences – one action follows another. Your evening sequence of events is likely to follow a particular order. Perhaps it includes walking the dog, organising dinner, setting the table, cleaning up, collapsing on the couch, preparing for the next day, putting kids to bed. It may be some of those tasks or others. Regardless, as you think back through a typical evening, I am sure much of it is predictable and follows a similar path.

Within *The Elite: Think like an athlete, succeed like a champion* I included a chapter on habit formation, such is its power in setting an athlete up for success. It details the steps required for habit formation. What I didn't include within that book is the way that we can influence the habits formed by others. Indeed, a helpful tool for parents and coaches.

The essence of habit formation is to understand those good intentions do not necessarily result in the desired action. This is the ultimate frustration of changing behaviours. We want to do it, but don't do it, and then blame ourselves for our lack of conviction or self-discipline. The truth is that most habit formation fails to occur because our minds are busy enough – we have too many things happening at once, and we don't think of it at the moment we need it. The solution that increases the likelihood of real and permanent change is to find a way to trigger the new behaviour, *on the back of something we already regularly do*. For example, let's say a teen athlete frequently arrives at training with things missing from their training bag which gets them in trouble from the coach. It sets the session off badly, the coach is annoyed, and the athlete feels unprepared. The challenge at the athletes' end is that they run in the door from school, grab their training bag and go. There isn't much time to check their bag that everything is in place. Where the window of opportunity is to get organised, may be the night before when the bag was put in the laundry.

Here is the phrasing that can work to get a new habit in place:

'Jack, I know you want to be organised when you get to training and you don't want coach to get cranky with you. From now on, *when* you take your bag to the laundry after training. *Then* unpack it and put in your gear for the next session.'

The two keywords in the advice are *when* and *then*. *When* and *then* are the contingencies that will connect the new habit to the pre-existing behaviour. The when is the trigger; it prompts someone to think that there was something to remember. The then becomes the consequence of the trigger. If you want to understand more about how this strategy works, my book *The Elite* summarises it for you. Mostly, you just need to know that a trigger with a consequence will increase the likelihood of behaviour change by approximately two to three times.

I must mention the fine print. My experience is that sadly this strategy does not work on wet towels on bedroom floors. When I tried, 'Boys, *when* you've finished drying yourself, *then* hang your towel up' it was sadly a dismal flop. Not because there was anything wrong with my phrasing. The when/then was great. The fine print is that you have to want to change the behaviour!

wysiwyg

Mental rehearsal and visualisation are evidence-based strategies that are used to improve performance, increase confidence, refine technique and prepare for competition. They are also particularly helpful for teens and athletes who are injured. In terms of how we see the performance, there is no difference between an actual experience and an imagined one. This means that your mind cannot tell the difference between a race that you run in-person and a race that you run within your mind. Visualisation works because neurons in our brains interpret imagery as equivalent to real-life action. When we visualise an activity, the brain generates an impulse that has the neurons 'perform' the movement.

There is an enormous difference in physicality from going for a run and sitting on the couch and thinking about it. However, there is much to be gained from visualising a well-executed run. Just as an actor must rehearse every line and gesture of an upcoming play, the athlete can mentally prepare for psychological aspects of their sport. Visualisation is the act of recreating the images, feelings and sounds within your mind of an activity, to practise it at a level of excellence. Visualisation offers physical benefits as a training effect, enhances confidence, maintains positivity and helps to improve performance.

If you've ever thought about making a mistake, and then made it – that was because you visualised it first. Visualisation is a powerful technique that sets the tone for the performance. Quite simply, What You See Is What You Get – WYSIWYG.

Don't just visualise the positive – expect the unexpected

Likewise, visualise positive and negative scenarios. Let's face it, no matter what the situation, sport always finds a way to challenge us. Your teen may tell you they can't get the image of making a mistake out of their head. An athlete once said to me, before a semi-final, 'Jo, I see myself running on the field, and I just know I'm going to pull my hamstring'. When we are caught up in negative images, and often this will be in times of higher anxiety or pressure, visualisation is a great strategy. Here's how the conversation went with that athlete:

Me	Have you been having some trouble with your hamstring?
Athlete	No.
Me	But when you imagine yourself in the game, the trouble pops up?
Athlete	Yes, I know that sounds weird, but I can't stop that thought.
Me	Ok, that can happen close to important games. I want you to take a breath (athlete took a breath) and tell me what it looks like when you're running strongly down the field, tell me what that looks like, describe great running to me.
Athlete	Well, I'm tall and strong, my stride is well balanced, and my arms are pumping, I'm putting myself into position to take the ball.
Me	What does that description feel like?
Athlete	Great.
Me	Negative images are really common close to a big game. That's ok, don't fight it. Just remember, *when* you have an unhelpful image, *then* see yourself doing the opposite. See yourself performing well, and your confidence will take over.

In this way, if your child tells you about something unhelpful that they can see or imagine, you can help them shift their thinking past it by:
1. Acknowledging the way they were thinking and normalise it.
2. Having them describe the more helpful, positive outcome.
3. If you're feeling adventurous, throw in a when/then like I did in the last comment, and you increase the likelihood that visualisation will become a habit.

Remember the footballer I described earlier who made the mistake with the high ball? Visualising catching it well was an important part of the intervention to get back to taking high ball catches.

You may find times when your teen worries about the 'what ifs'. The things that could go wrong, no matter how likely or unlikely they may be. It can be helpful if they plan a possible solution and visualise themselves overcoming it.

For example:
- cramps
- being ahead
- being behind
- blisters
- wardrobe malfunction
- problems with nutrition
- weather – too hot, too cold, rain, wind.

Visualise what you can control.
Focusing on the controllable has already been discussed within the book, and visualisation is a great strategy to combine with it. Visualising executing a race plan, going through the warm-up routine, and even focusing on the breath. By directing thinking to those physical and mental aspects that can be controlled, the

nerves will become manageable, and the likelihood of excellent performance will increase.

A tip sheet on visualisation is available at the following link: https://www.drjolukins.com/in-the-grandstands

confidence? check!

I have had athletes approach me for advice or strategies to enhance personal confidence. Confidence is an important part of who we are. When I ask athletes what confidence will look like for them, they often reply that they don't know, but they will know it when they feel it.

Sometimes tricky to define, often difficult to measure yet crucially important in the success and enjoyment experienced by an athlete through their sport.

One day an athlete, Melissa approached me with this very question. Melissa was seeking reassurance for her ability to perform at the next level of competition – she had just been selected in the next tier of competition and was simultaneously delighted and horrified!

As I often do, I asked Melissa what confidence would mean to her and precisely how things would be different if she felt confident. Melissa struggled to articulate what that would be other than she knew it wasn't how she was currently feeling. I could see in this instance, Melissa was struggling to put her finger on the cause of her worry, so I decided to take another tact.

I had recently read a research article on key principles that athletes had identified as elements of confidence. I was able to talk to Melissa about the principles and following the appointment returned to the article and converted the key points to a checklist. I have included the checklist on the next page. This checklist is available for download at https://www.drjolukins.com/in-the-grandstands

Pending the age of the athlete, it might be a document they can work through themselves or in discussion with their coach. In this case, I worked through the checklist with Melissa. I told her that the checklist included key indicators of confidence, and by working through the list, it would help her to keep on track in building her confidence.

Interestingly there were some items Melissa felt could be ticked off straight away (like a commitment to success and training) and others to work on. Of course, the checklist didn't bring Melissa confidence. What it did was offer a framework through which to view confidence and a sense of progress and tracking towards a goal. The end of the story came after a few weeks of Melissa revisiting the list until she got to the point that her improved confidence was evident, and the list was not mentioned again!

Confidence Check List

- COMMITMENT
- QUALITY TRAINING
- CLEAR GOALS
- VISUALISATION
- MINDFULNESS
- RACE PLANS
- RECIPE?
- MANAGING DISTRACTION
- EVALUATION

how a mental skills coach can help

A mental skills coach is sometimes recruited to assist an athlete or a coach as part of the sporting journey. Our years of training, focusing specifically on the mental side of the sport, can certainly bring value to an athlete's sporting experience. The key factor I have always found helpful to families is that I can help to understand the underlying factors that need to be addressed because I am not intricately involved in their lives. Being able to sit outside of their family and sporting dynamics and not having a personal relationship with them allows me to assess the situation far more objectively and in a way that will help. I am not vested in the family, other than to help them.

Does your child need to consult with a mental skills coach? Maybe. It's certainly not what will suit all children or all families. It also adds a further financial load that may not be possible for some families. If your teen is heading down the elite pathway, it can certainly be considered. Much of it will depend upon how they are navigating that journey, how well they are coping, whether they are managing any worries within or outside their sport, and their mental game when competing.

It's at this point that I will shout out to all the coaches involved with our teen athletes. They are coaching both the physical and mental elements of teen sport and may be just the right balance of what the athlete needs. No specific mental skills coach required. I have worked in the elite athlete domain for nearly 30 years and for the majority of those who are 18 years and over, I am the first person with sport psychology training they have worked with. Most high-level athletes get towards the pointy end of high-level performance without working with a sport psychologist.

Employing a mental skills coach is certainly not a requirement for your child to attain at the elite level – however, it can in some instances, help. Sometimes a child need only work through a small block, perhaps they become overwhelmed with worry before the competition, or they can't sleep the night before a big game. If talking with parents and coaches doesn't resolve it, you may find benefit in having them read something in the area (here's where I cheekily recommend my book, *The Elite: Think like an athlete, succeed like a champion*), or a consultation with a mental skills coach in your area may be helpful.

I have developed a package of mental skills training for athletes: simply explained, self-paced and easily delivered online. See https://www.drjolukins.com/in-the-grandstands for the link and for a special discount as an *In the Grandstands* reader!

IN THE PAIN: COPING WITH INJURY

CHAPTER 5

Injury taught me I need to learn how to face challenges.
Shawn Johnson

A COMMON EXPERIENCE THROUGH sport is injury. Whether it be short-term complaints that need to be tolerated through training or performance, or substantive that involve considerable time from the sport, injury can challenge even the most resilient of athletes. It is unusual to be the parent of a teen athlete, and not at some stage be the parent of an injured teen athlete.

Typical injuries include bruises, sprains, strains and fractures. Contact sports will also often see head and neck injuries. Whatever the injury, time away from their sport is likely to have a psychological impact in addition to the physical effects.

more than skin-deep

The impact of an injury can be substantial, beyond the physical injury itself. Parents need to understand that a teen with an injury that disrupts their life may have any of the following reactions:

'I've been an athlete all my life. If I can't do this, then who am I?'
'The team needs me, and I'm letting them down by not being able to play.'
'Being physical helps me blow off; it's how I cope when I'm stressed. What will I do now?'
'All my friends are part of my sport. I feel alone.'
'My dreams are gone.'
'I feel like I've lost my confidence.'

The sense of loss, whether real or imagined, is impactful for some athletes. These feelings can be strong and powerful and coping through these times is an important time of learning for our teenage athletes.

the importance of attitude

The attitude of an athlete is crucial to the rehabilitation process. Having worked in the elite athlete domain for three decades, I have seen firsthand the impact of injury, and the critical influence mindset has on recovery and return. My PhD research explored the injury experience of elite rugby league footballers. That research explored several key questions, one being the influence of mindset on recovery. For two years we recorded injury data on more than 50 players competing at the national level. Also, we kept data on the psychological mindset of players before, during and post-injury.

I can recall the meeting with the head coach to report the initial findings. I was detailing the average number of injuries sustained per player through the seasons and the average number of days an injury would keep them from playing. I hadn't got too far when he pulled me up to ensure I had considered the data according to playing position. Within rugby league, it would generally be expected that more injuries would be sustained by forwards than backs. A forward in rugby league is responsible for taking the ball forward for the team and typically sustains the majority of the high impact collisions. The backs form more of the playmaker role and work to the line after the forwards have gained the momentum.

If you only compared data for injury according to playing position, it revealed what you might expect. Forwards typically sustained more injuries across a season than backs. The fascinating finding within the research was revealed when the variable of attitude was considered. I had included a measure of attributional style into the project.

Essentially attributional style measures how an athlete 'explains the world' and those explanations can then be categorised more broadly into whether the athlete is optimistic or pessimistic. An optimist views the world through possibility. They will tend to assume a positive outcome, expect things to go well, primarily to see that every cloud has a silver lining. In contrast, a pessimist gravitates towards viewing the world through a negative lens. They expect adverse outcomes, they are heavy on blame, and they notice that for every silver lining will be a cloud.

What difference then did this make for the injured footballers? An important one. Attributional style explained the injury experience better than playing position! An optimistic forward spent less time away from playing than a pessimistic back. The mindset of the athlete influenced recovery time in a way that playing position couldn't explain.

The way you think matters. An optimistic mindset, in part, explains the recovery process when an injury occurs. This makes sense, as the self-talk of an athlete directly impacts on their emotional experience. Emotions are the aspect of us that drives our behaviour. To contrast the two mindsets:

	Optimist	**Pessimist**
Situation	The athlete has a torn bicep	The athlete has a torn bicep
Self-talk	'I need to do all my rehab, the better I work at that and get it done, the sooner I'll get back to playing.'	'This sucks. I don't think this will ever heal. It doesn't matter what I do. This is the worst.'
Emotions	Determined and motivated	Frustrated and hopeless
Behaviour	Is compliant with the rehabilitation program. Does exercises as required.	Partially compliant with rehabilitation recovers slower than expected and is quite harmful through the experience.

The same torn bicep results in two very different outcomes dependent upon how the event is interpreted. Self-talk is a commentary we have going in our heads all of the time. Whether we are young or young at heart, our voice travels with us. Our children develop their self-talk through their experiences, and their experiences develop through their self-talk.

How you react when you experience adversity matters. What you say out loud will influence how they understand reactions to events. It is why we often see similar patterns in reactions pass down through generations.

ways to support your teen through injuries

Get an excellent support team around you. Whether that be a doctor, physiotherapist, podiatrist, psychologist, exercise physiologist, masseuse or other health professional, a multi-disciplinary team can be a great network to support your teen when they are injured, but also to prepare them in their training and prehab to reduce the risk of injury.

Express love and empathy. This is a time of hurt – both physical and emotional – and children need the love and support of their parents. Share with them that you are there to help them understand what they are going through. The key things required from you are the things that are always needed by your child: tell them you love them, show physical affection and reassure them.

Keep communication up. Where you can, encourage your child to talk about what they are thinking or feeling and acknowledge what they express. It's ok to be sad or angry, scared or apprehensive. They are normal emotions to feel; however, we want to ensure they don't get stuck within them. Acknowledging the emotion first is the starting point for moving through. It doesn't help if you dismiss it ('It's not that bad') or make false promises ('Everything will be ok').

Ensure you are allowing your teen to make decisions. Let them participate actively around their treatment options. It is very easy in a medical system to slip into the role of patient and have little control over the decision-making process. Remember that perceiving there is little control is unhelpful for most athletes. Keeping athletes involved in the process, explaining the options and letting them make decisions (where possible) is the best approach.

Treat the recovery like sport. Rethinking the rehabilitation process can be a helpful way forward. Thinking of it as a challenge to overcome and developing a 'game plan' might be useful. With the assistance of the supervising medical team, determine an outcome goal (e.g. when back to training or competing), specify the process goals (e.g. exercises, hydro, strapping) and use that as motivation.

Keep your teen involved with the team or sport. One of the most significant challenges of sustaining an injury is feeling like part of your identity has been lost. Explore with your teen and their coach ways in which they can stay involved with their sport. Is there a behind the scenes role they can play, like keeping particular stats at games? Perhaps they can sit on the bench or still attend practice or meetings. There may be another athlete in the team who is injured, and they can work together. All of these options would require consultation with your teen but may be helpful as a part of their recovery. It is also likely to help them when they return to play, by keeping up with what is happening within the team/sport, strategies, games, etc. Visualisation is a further way to keep engaged with the competition, whether it be focusing on a technique or visualising a plan or new play.

Plan the road. There can be unknowns in the timing of recovery, however, where you can, encourage your teen to focus on the treatment and what is within their control during this time. When it feels hard, or they are discouraged, acknowledge that. It is essential they feel understood. These thoughts and feelings are usually transient; they come and go. However, if they appear 'stuck', then help from a professional might be helpful.

Share the road. Injury can take time. It can be frustrating and at times, lonely. Reassuring your child, they can count on you for support and assistance will be valuable throughout their recovery.

Where you can, learn about the injury so you can assist in the decision making. Be real in your assessment of their situation; don't promise what you don't know and be positive and optimistic where you can.

Watch for the warning signs. If any of the following are persistent and intense within your teen, consider getting external support.

- Ongoing denial or disbelief – 'It's not that bad' when it is.
- Strong and consistent feelings of anger or sadness.
- Withdrawal from family, friends or disengagement from other activities.
- Sudden refusal to comply with treatment.
- Coping in unhelpful ways (e.g. substance abuse).

returning from injury

Returning from injury will require some consideration. Depending upon the injury, it may be that advice from a physiotherapist or sports physician regarding the return, be attended to, and your teen returns to their sport. Alternatively depending upon the nature of the injury or how it was sustained, it may mean there is some hesitation or worry by your teen. This is a meaningful conversation and not something to be dismissed with a, 'Don't be silly, you'll be fine'.

Start by asking your teen what their concerns are. If they are worried about the possibility of re-injury, some advice and reassurance from a medical professional may be helpful. You might need to help them to phrase the question, 'Doc, I know that I've done all the rehab, but I'm worried about re-injuring my knee. What is the likelihood that it will happen again? Is my knee strong enough to return?'

If they are getting repetitive negative images of re-injury or the initial injury, this can be addressed with some imagery work of doing the task well. For example, visualising:

- making a strong tackle
- jumping to catch the ball and landing well
- spinning and stopping sharply
- performing a layup through traffic and scoring the basket.

For further information on visualisation, refer back to p.68.

career over

This is tough, particularly in the early career of a young athlete. Any athlete who has their career end unexpectedly is likely to be significantly challenged. The grief reaction was described earlier with regards to other disappointments. As a reminder, grief to any loss can trigger feelings of disbelief, denial, anger, anxiety, frustration, depression and eventually understanding and acceptance. In terms of behaviours, we may witness tears, withdrawal, lashing out, need for comfort, compliance, and non-compliance.

It is essential to understand that in addition to the reaction of our teen, it is the reactions that we in the family also hold that is important. I was once wisely told that to be a parent is to walk around with your heart permanently outside your body. When something happens to our children, to some extent, it also happens to us. We are likely to experience our own grief response. We need to recognise this for two key reasons. The first is that all the emotions and behaviours described above may be our experiences too. The second is that our reaction to this outcome is going to influence our response (whether we recognise that or not).

It's normal to grieve; in fact, it's helpful. Pushing emotion to one side, pretending we aren't distressed when we are, none of that helps us to move through an experience. The other thing for our teen that can be helpful is to see that there are times when we don't hold it all together. When we can be honest with our feelings and share our distress, it helps our children to understand that we aren't superheroes and vulnerability is part of being human. That being said, it is also helpful for us to role model coping, and so there is a balance for us in travelling through the grief experience to someone else's loss.

I have been involved with teens who have taken the injury that triggers the end of a sporting career or level of competition, a particularly hard way. I have seen athletes who have experienced severe depression and have expressed uncertainty about living a life that does not include their sport. These situations should always be taken seriously. If your child has expressed such concerns, they need to know you have heard them and you need to take action. It is beyond the scope of this book to step you through a scenario as severe as this and I would always start with a visit to a trusted GP to start the conversation as to what support and necessary interventions can be put in place. I will repeat, this is a conversation that needs attention and advice without delay.

IN THE SMILE: KEEPING IT FUN

CHAPTER 6

Never, ever underestimate the importance of having fun.
Randy Pausch

CAST YOUR MIND BACK to when your child first started playing sport. Remember how little they were! Perhaps their uniform was two sizes too big, perhaps their soccer team resembled a swarm of bees all hovering around the ball. Can you remember the look on their face when they finished and came running back to you to tell you all about it? There's every chance that they did so with a massive smile on their face. This is the most important lesson for athletes and parents in what sport offers the most. Sport offers fun.

fun comes first

While many young children pay attention to the outcome of their sport – after all, we do keep score of goals, who was first to the finish or who stood on the podium – many young children don't place the same importance on it as adults do. Most team sports deliberately don't hold finals series until children reach the early teenage years. This is done specifically to keep the focus on the enjoyment of the sport itself rather than the pressure of winning or losing.

The shift in emphasis from fun to winning is a likely reason for much of the drop out in sport. Interestingly when you ask young athletes what 'fun' is during sport, they don't tell me it's mucking around or joking. A fascinating study by Amanda Visek and colleagues investigated what youth athletes say makes the sport fun. They came up with 81 reasons! These were then summarised to 11 key factors that described fun in sport for kids.

The most important (explaining more than 30% of what children find fun) were:
1. Positive team dynamics
2. Trying hard
3. Positive coaching

The remaining 70% came from the following (in order)
4. Learning and improving
5. Game time support
6. Games
7. Practice
8. Team friendships
9. Mental bonuses
10. Team rituals

And, the least important
11. Swag (e.g. travelling, or having a cool uniform).

The importance of this research is that winning featured in the bottom category. While children like winning, it is generally considered to be one of the lowest predictors of fun and one of the least likely incentives to keep most kids 'in the game'.

At the elite level, the outcome matters. Vast sums of money are spent within sports, people make it their careers, and few athletes attend the Olympics purely, 'for the fun of it'. This is the pointy end, and the whole world may be watching. This does not mean that fun doesn't play a critical role in the playing experience and outcome of sport for many athletes.

I have worked with world-class athletes and can confidently attest that having fun has a serious role to play within the minds of elite performers. When elite athletes have been fortunate to train and play an entire career, much of what keeps them showing up in the last few years of their sport is how much they enjoy it. I have had athletes who have been paid large sums of money tell me it isn't enough to keep them training and playing when it stops being fun.

fun and dropout

Of concern is that around 70% of children have dropped out of sport by 13 years of age. The health impacts this has for us as a community makes it a significant issue. There is usually a range of reasons why this is the case. However, the most commonly expressed reason by teens for dropping out is, it's not fun anymore.

This is critical for coaches and parents to remember in scheduling teens through training and competition. One of the reasons we bring players together for a muck-around game of cricket on game-day within professional rugby league is to get the players moving and doing something fun and a guaranteed laugh. Not surprisingly, they still manage to take this reasonably competitively – all while having fun.

Unfortunately, longevity in sport is often not consistent with our expectations. The following results came from a comprehensive study by the Robert Wood Johnson Foundation. While 75% of adults indicate they have participated in youth sport, only 25% are still playing after the age of 25 years. When you ask parents the likelihood their children will still be participating as adults, 72% indicate it is likely. Losing sight of what keeps our children motivated and engaged is the most likely reason they will stop playing.

Interestingly the top two reasons adults indicated they played sports were for personal enjoyment and health. Hmm, adults. We sound a lot like big kids! Let's keep fun well and truly on the radar of the sporting experience.

fun as an intervention

Similarly, when I have had athletes hit 'flat patches' in their career, the aspects of enjoyment and fun are always part of the discussion. Times when athletes are underperforming with no physical explanation, I will always consider the presence (or absence) of fun as part of the discussion. All athletes need to keep in touch with what is fun for them about their sport as that will sustain them and help them to perform at their best. I realise that it can go both ways, and when it's not fun, performance can drop. Similarly, when performance drops its usually not fun. Rather than think of this as a chicken-and-egg scenario, it highlights the importance of fun and re-exploring fun whenever possible.

A conversation about what they enjoy most, and what about their sport makes them smile can be helpful to put the important value of enjoyment back into the centre of the sport. Fun, is serious business!

why does fun make a difference?

Fun is not only enjoyable, it also enhances physical and psychological wellbeing. When we're enjoying ourselves, endorphins are increased in the body which decreases stress and improves our pain tolerance. We manage our relationships more effectively and are better company to be around. Importantly, fun lifts our energy levels, helps our bodies to relax and release tension and makes us more creative in our decision-making.

Its benefits are also evident when we look through the lens of anxiety and tension. Worry, being the opposite of fun, does not prepare you well mentally and physically for performance. It is the same whether you are an adult or a child. When we are enjoying ourselves, we are more likely to relax and be mentally prepared for what is ahead. Should sport *always be fun?* Wouldn't that be nice! Sadly, no. Anything worth achieving comes from a basis of effort and work. There are times in the middle of 'the slog' that fun would be the last word we'd use to describe it. The thought that every moment will be a joy is an illusion.

As important as it is to value fun, it's important to recognise that there is something to be gained from working hard, pushing through and finishing something despite the discomfort, or knowledge that the task wasn't pleasant. If we over-emphasise fun, we miss the reality that sometimes worthwhile things have an element of the unpleasant.

I have met many teens who have not learnt this lesson. Those who think everything should be fun, and life should only be filled with activities that bring joy and purpose are heading down the road of disappointment. They have learnt this living in an environment where the purpose is emphasised but the foundations of effort and the grind to get you there is not. Sometimes we do things in sport (repetitive drills, gym sessions, time trials) that athletes might describe as a long way from fun. The importance of pushing through these activities is two-fold. They certainly have a purpose to the ultimate goal, and they help to build resilience to tolerate things that we don't like.

Fun is incredibly important. It helps to have it on our radar. In addition, doing things which are unpleasant, unpalatable, un-fun (I know, not a word, but go with me on that one!) also serve a purpose and help us to be grateful for the fun when it arrives.

how can you emphasise the value of fun?

When your child knows you place value on fun, it can go a long way to developing it as a value for them. Remember the importance of the questions you ask. If your first question is, 'Did you win?' they will learn the importance of winning as a value for you. From the question, 'Did you have fun?' the emphasis of enjoyment will be clear.

- Remember that the understanding of fun varies, and enjoyment can be derived from things that are not immediately apparent.
- Focusing on what can be improved allows for autonomy and an increased sense of control.
- Foster the love of a challenge. A teen will shy away from a challenge if they are worried about how you see failure. If you respond with positive encouragement, it makes an effort the focus more so than the outcome.
- Have a sense of humour and laugh often.
- Role model fun within your own life, laugh at challenges when they come along and don't go the way you wanted. Your child will learn much from your reactions.
- Fun is an inherent part of childhood and teen life. Our children must have the opportunity to incorporate it into their life experiences, particularly within their sport.

IN THE HEART: WHY GRATITUDE MATTERS

CHAPTER 7

Gratitude and fear can't stand the sight of each other.
Robin Sharma

GRATITUDE HAS BECOME RECOGNISED as an essential element of wellbeing for people of all ages. Now integrated into many school pastoral care programs, the impact gratitude has on enhancing our lives and reducing our stress and worries has received welcome prominence. When exploring the variables which improve wellbeing, gratitude features prominently.

For this reason, I have included gratitude as a standalone topic in lectures within the Positive Psychology component of a course I teach to university students. While appreciation might appear at first glance to be a warm and fuzzy concept; there is hard science to support its value in human experience and endeavour. With this focus, I have specifically been interested to see the progression of research into the role of gratitude in enhancing sporting performance.

positive benefits of gratitude

Athletes who approach their training and performance with a mindset of gratitude demonstrate an attitude (or experience the feeling) of benefit. From the Latin word gratus, it is considered to be 'pleasing' or 'thankful'. When someone is grateful, they have a readiness to show appreciation for and to return kindness. An athlete might be thankful for the opportunity to participate in their sport or thankful for a coach for coaching them. Also, they may be pleased to have overcome an injury and be returning to their competition.

Interesting research on gratitude has found:

⇒ Gratitude enhances positive changes in an athlete's self-esteem (Chen & Wu, 2014)
⇒ Appreciation improved attitude, awareness, capacity to deal with stress, and enhanced performance in Olympic athletes (Howells & Fitzallen, 2019)
⇒ Practising gratitude can lead to improved quality of sleep and reduced psychological distress (Gabana, 2019).'

the mechanism of gratitude

The act of being thankful is one of the most impactful things you can do to reduce symptoms of stress, increase happiness and enhance your performance. When we are grateful, we stop to reflect on what we appreciate. It could be about the people in our lives, the opportunities we have, the possessions that we own or the lifestyle we are afforded. Finding moments of gratitude in our day is an excellent way to reduce feelings of stress and worry, particularly in the busy nature of a day at school. Sometimes described as the 'social glue' that forms relationships, it is a central element to a well-functioning society.

The considered question is to ask how gratitude and performance are related. As a way of thinking, recognition causes a shift in our mental focus. When thinking moves *towards* appreciation, it consequently moves *away* from unhappiness, resentment and anger. I bluntly point out in workshops that you can't be grateful at the same time as whingeing or complaining.

Further research by Brown and Wong (2017) showed that people who are primed for gratitude, that is they have a continuous focus on appreciation, will demonstrate changes to the prefrontal cortex. It seems that you can train your brain to be more receptive to expressing gratitude.

self-control and gratitude

In fairness to our children, self-control is tricky enough for adults, so self-regulating when you're young can be a big ask! Regardless, great habits start early and so reinforcing self-control at a young age can have significant benefits in the long term. The questions we ask ourselves after training or competition can reinforce self-control.

'What felt good today?' is a valuable question, as it turns the focus on positivity and wellbeing. The answer may be about a part of the technique, teamwork or the exhilaration of movement. Whatever it is, the question 'What felt good today?' emphasises the training session or competition from a grateful approach.

A further question that emphasises self-control is 'How could I improve next time?'. This question is reflective of a growth mindset and acknowledges the opportunity of learning and the benefit of self-reflection. Athletes who pause and reflect on future improvement will build on their current abilities and set themselves on the path of development and performance.

the power of what you get to do

When people speak of their daily activities, it is often phrased through the things they have to do. 'I *have to* make my bed', 'I *have to* unstack the dishwasher', or 'I *have to* go to school'. Athletes are no different. 'I *have to* go to training', 'I *have to* go to bed early', or 'I *have to* do my stretches'. It's the same for parents. 'I *have* to do school pick up', 'I *have* to drive the kids to training', 'I *have* to cook dinner'.

It sounds taxing like it's a lot of effort, and there may be moments where it feels exhausting. However, the reality is that athletes are choosing to do their sport. When working with elite athletes, I overwhelmingly hear that if given a choice, they would not do anything else.

'Have to' sounds like an obligation and is often considered in a negative way. But what happens if you change the phrasing? Instead of thinking of tasks as an obligation enforced upon you, find them from a sense of gratitude and appreciation? This subtle (yet significant) difference is possible by changing the things that *have* to be done to something that we *get* to do.

Perhaps it is now, I:
- get to go to school (versus those who don't have access to education)
- get to do chores at home (versus those who are homeless)
- get to go to training (versus those who are injured)
- get to work hard at training (versus those who aren't being pushed to improve)
- get to pack up from training (versus those who don't have resources).

I once worked with a group of elite athletes, assisting them to incorporate gratitude into their training and competition. One team member was injured. He observed that in his time away from training, he so desperately wanted to be back in the gym and training alongside his teammates. However, he knew (from previous experience) that it would probably only take a week back and he would return to the mindset of being negative going to training, seeing it as a chore. Through the group conversation, the lightbulb moment occurred for him, and he realised he needed to find a way to look at training through the lens of gratitude.

This is the skill that our children can benefit from in so many ways. Gratitude is a game-changer. To travel through life understanding how many opportunities we have, how wonderful the people in our lives can be, and all the very many things we have to be thankful for is a life skill. Gratitude is consistent with a positive mindset, and the evidence is overwhelming for the benefits this holds for us in terms of wellbeing and happiness.

The extra nugget of gold for athletes is that gratitude is a **performance enhancer.**

using gratitude to reach goals

Being aware of mindset and gratitude through training can add resiliency when undertaking challenging training sessions. When you are thankful for the opportunity to swim, or grateful for being able to go to practice and focus on improving performance, it makes it a little bit easier to head out to training on a cold morning or in the sweltering heat.

Beyond the added resiliency, being actively focused on what you have (and savouring it) lends itself to more productive goal setting. The goals of a grateful athlete are more likely to be centred around performance and personal growth than those benchmarks that rely on other people or circumstances.

Gratitude is much like motivation, in that it can be both a fleeting feeling and a consistent personality characteristic. It is undoubtedly the case that someone who regularly practises and observes gratitude is more likely to create a regular habit of being appreciative. One of the best ways for our children to learn appreciation is to live in an environment where it is valued. Listen out within your household. If there is whingeing and complaining, it doesn't leave much room for gratitude. Indeed, it is ok to acknowledge those things that are not ok and work to improve them but always leave space to be appreciative for what goes well or what we can be thankful for.

gratitude in disguise

The beauty of gratitude is that it can be embraced and discussed without having to use the word gratitude. An essential distinction in defining gratitude is in understanding what it is not. Gratitude is not complaining and whingeing. I have yet to find an athlete who can express appreciation for their circumstances or experiences at the same time that they are ungrateful.

Take for example, when something doesn't go to plan, it's raining during competition. Yes, this is an uncontrollable event that affects both your child's experience and the opposing athletes. The truth is, it can be an excellent opportunity to practise dealing with something that is both unpleasant and out of your control. So in the instance, your child says, 'It sucks that it's raining', you can steer the conversation to gratitude by first acknowledging what they have said and then having them reflect on the upside, 'It would be nice if it weren't raining. However, given that it is, how can you use it to your advantage?' Their answer may focus on the task, 'It's a good chance to practise my ball skills in the wet', or focus on their thoughts, 'It can help me block out weather and focus on playing'.

This thought conversion strategy is a winner for refining mindset. It takes you from a place of complaint to an appreciation of your circumstances. Physiologically this helps to relax the body and will enhance performance. While this is a strategy for your child to develop, it is useful for you to think through a few examples, so you are prepared when these conversations come up.

Adversity	Comment by child	Acknowledgment & Prompt	Reframe
It's hot	'It's too hot; I don't feel like doing this.'	'It is hot out there. How can this prepare you for the game up north next month?'	'Well it will probably be hotter up north, so this is a chance to practise my hydration.'
The coach benched your child	'Coach doesn't like me.'	'It's disappointing not to play, and sometimes it's difficult when you don't know why. What might you be able to do to increase your chances of play more next time?'	'Everyone has some time on the bench. If I talk to the coach, I might be able to find ways to get better.'
Your child didn't get the PB they hoped for	'It's not fair; I should have got that.'	'It can feel unfair when we don't get what we've been working for. What happened today that you can use to improve at the next carnival?'	'My start wasn't good. Maybe I just need to work on that some more.'
They lost	'That sucks, I hate losing.'	'Losing doesn't often feel fun. Given we can't change that, how can you find something positive for next time?'	'Well, I know I'm not going to use that play again. I guess it tells me that it didn't work, and I need to find another way.'

A vital part of the success of the conversation will come from the acknowledgment of what the child has said. This can be challenging when, as a parent, your child says something that sounds unreasonable to you. Regardless, the best way to move forward is to acknowledge what your child has said (without requiring you to agree with them). Doing so will tell them that you heard them, and will help to direct them towards a more helpful, and grateful mindset.

thank you to the opposition

It is common for athletes to experience anxiety or worry about the capabilities of their opposition competitors or teams. I have found gratitude to be a helpful intervention in anxiety management and to shift the focus of performance away from others and back to self.

Imagine an athlete has participated in a competition, and there was an opposition player/team who was particularly skilled. It is common for an athlete to react to this by comparing themselves negatively to the opposition. This heightens concern and worry and harms self-belief. Gratitude can help productively shift this thinking through a specific question: *What is the upside of competing against this high standard?*

The answers can include:
- 'It helped me to see the standard firsthand.'
- 'I had to raise my level to compete against them.'
- 'I'm at a level to compete against them.'

The standard of others is a variable we cannot control. Our reaction to it, however, is firmly within our domain. If rather than viewing others and criticising ourselves in comparison, we recognise our potential and the opportunity, it helps us to embrace the situation better. We will gain more from it. It would be like playing in the NBA in the days of Jordan, Pippen and Shaq. How awesome would that have been! Being grateful for the opportunity is a much better way to enjoy the experience rather than taking a contrary negative view.

IN THE MIRROR: LEADING BY EXAMPLE

CHAPTER 8

> Every interaction with our children is a reflection of our own relationship with ourselves.
>
> **Dr Shefali**

Now it's our turn.

BUT WAIT, ISN'T THIS book about our children? Absolutely, and enhancing our relationship with our children means that we need a good understanding of who we are as people and as parents. I need to qualify that I am not a parenting expert. I have however, been a parent for 18 years, so I know what it is to walk around with your heart outside your body. I have made plenty of mistakes. Plenty. They could probably stand alone as a separate book!

The good news is there isn't a formula from which an ideal parenting style emerges. Everyone has their style and beliefs, and so we each need to find an approach that works for our families and us, as best we can. We will make mistakes, absolutely, and then we need to find ways to forgive ourselves and learn when that happens. Some guidelines and principles can be useful as we navigate the parenting responsibility, probably one of the boldest tasks we will ever take on! Therefore, I will share what I know, both from my experience as a parent, from working alongside other parents and from what I have come to know and understand by reading the relevant research in the parenting domain.

Let's pause and look in the mirror.

what sort of parent am I?

A vital place to start is to ask yourself who you are as a parent. How you approach parenting, feel about your parenting style, and if there are aspects of your parenting style, you would like to change. This can be a useful practice across all aspects of parenting. To gain a valuable reflection of your parenting style, you may want to ask yourself the following questions or to download the handout from this link: https://www.drjolukins.com/in-the-grandstands.

1. List examples of parenting behaviours in your child's sport you don't like. This can be from other parents, friends or strangers. Put an asterisk next to any actions you notice you have done in the past.
2. List examples of parenting behaviours in the sport you do like. Again, asterisk what you do in your parenting.
3. Ask yourself questions about why you do or don't like the behaviours from lists one and two. The *why* question will help you to understand the values you have about parenting in sport.
4. Finally, consider what would help you improve your parenting behaviour. Create a plan of action for future occurrences.

It's essential as we reflect on our parenting, that we do so observing what we do, without judging what we do. It can be a tough enough journey at times making decisions and hoping we are making the best ones for the time and place, without placing a layer of judgement, criticism or guilt over our actions as well.

Our parenting is enhanced when we are aware of our actions, thoughts and behaviours. Spending some time reflecting on how we parent, what we do and don't like and how we might improve is an integral part of our parenting journey.

As I mentioned at the beginning of this book, Matt Williams OAM, once said, 'A good day is a good day and a bad day is a great story'. It is undoubtedly helpful to think that our parenting histories are full of good days and great stories!

what was your sporting journey?

Spend a few moments now travelling back in time, back to when you were at school, back to your teenage years. Remember who you were. I wonder what your aspirations were, who the significant people were in your life? Can you remember what you hoped for, your goals and what you dreaded most? Reflecting on our younger selves can make us feel vulnerable. The teenage years can feel awkward and uncertain, as well as hopeful and optimistic. The age and vulnerability that your child may be living through right now.

If we were having a conversation and you were telling me about your sporting journey as a teen, what would you tell me? Were you a success? Did you try hard and not reach your potential? Were you not involved in sports? What were the opportunities you wish you had and didn't? What were your other interests? What were they and were those experiences positive for you? Whatever your answers, whatever your skills, they all matter in terms of your child's sporting journey. What defines you can sharply define your child. It is worthy of your attention.

With your mind anchored in the past, it can be helpful to reflect on your sporting journey. I have seen well-intentioned parents put unnecessary pressure on their children to succeed either because:

    a. The parent was once successful within the sport and wants the same for their child, or

    b. The parent did not reach their perceived potential and wants their child to be more successful than they were.

chip off the old block

We are now heading into some delicate territory. Specifically, our relationship with our children and what their behaviour says about *us*.

We've all been there. They were young and in the playground; it was your child who pulled someone else's hair, pushed somebody over, snatched a toy or had a severe meltdown that caused everyone to stop and stare. Where did your self-talk head to? For many parents, probably most parents, it spent some time in, 'What does everyone else think, about me?' That is the moment where it felt like the whole world was watching. It felt like they were judging you. If you know that feeling, you're not alone.

It is understandable that we may feel our children's actions are, a reflection of us, and our parenting. When teenagers engage in inappropriate or illegal behaviour, one debate questions whether parents might even hold any sort of legal responsibility (and subsequent punishment) for such action. In some parts of the US, parents can be fined if children are out past the city curfew.

Within the sporting realm, we may lose sight of where the boundaries of our children's behaviours lie, and our responsibility begins. This can occur when our child does something inappropriate (like swearing at a referee) or fantastic (like scoring the game-winning goal). How much of that do you think is a reflection of you?

Psychology research and practice are clear that the parent-child relationship is critical. The style adopted by a parent and the attachment of the child goes a long way to explain the importance of values learned by a child. The research also highlights that innumerable other factors influence children.

What does this mean for parents in sport?

When your child makes a *poor decision* (for example, physically lashes out at someone, responds disrespectfully to a coach, has a strong reaction to not performing well), the critical consideration for you is how you conduct yourself in response. As parents, we lay the foundations, but we cannot take responsibility for our children's choices. When they make a poor choice, it is up to us to appropriately respond and be evident in the messaging of the learning. We don't need to take responsibility for their reaction, but we do need to be accountable for ours.

When your child attains an excellent *outcome* (for example, scores the winning point, or finishes well in front of the opposition) by all means clap, applaud, smile and cheer. Remember though that it was them in the arena and the outcome is theirs. Let them enjoy it, but be sure to let the success be theirs, just as the disappointments will be. If your child learns you invest a part of you into their success, it can unhelpfully add pressure for them.

Feels like a fine line to tread, and I would agree that it is. Please remember that your child will not always get it right, they won't always be consistent, make the ideal decision, or do what you expect. The best you can do is to be the soft place to land when their world crashes around them and understand that if you are doing your best, then most likely, it is enough. As a parent, your responses to their behaviours will be their best teacher. A few years ago, I attended a college ice hockey game in Canada. I took a photograph of this sign in the stadium, and revisit it often.

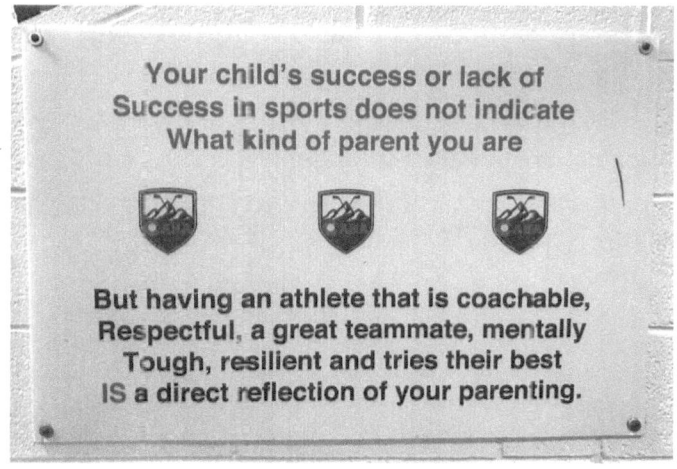

you as a role model

Many adult figures (coaches, teachers, extended family, adult family friends) serve as role models to influence a child's behaviour. However, parents remain the most significant figures of adult influence on the development of a child. Parents who support their child's sport through financial, practical and psychological support are likely to have a significant role in influencing their sports participation.

Our children have been watching and learning from us since they were born. Our behaviour concerning sport and exercise will speak more to our children than our words ever will. If we say, 'Be a good sport,' then we need to be one too. Children seem to have a sophisticated radar for calling out hypocrisy. Have you ever told your children to tidy up after themselves, only to have them point out to you the glass you left on the coffee table?! They will watch your actions, and so we need to be aware that our messages of good health, regular exercise, stretching, making better decisions, getting enough sleep and using self-discipline will be heard with a much more willing ear if they've seen you do it.

If this resonates as an area you can improve, you are in good company. Around 40% of what we do occurs on autopilot. Humans are creatures of habit, and so it is easy to slip into regular behaviours. Some work for us, others don't. If you would like to improve your patterns, I have resources that will help on my website. Creating powerful habits are good for us and good for our families.

For website resources on habits visit https://www.drjolukins.com/the-elite

the curious observer

What we ignore, controls us. Therefore, there is a great value that comes from paying attention to your thoughts and feelings. One of the best ways to helpfully self-reflect is to ask yourself 'What' questions more so than 'Why' questions. 'What am I feeling right now?' or 'What did I just say to myself?' are the types of items that can keep us curious. In contrast, 'Why am I feeling upset?' or 'Why am I always so negative?' is likely to take us into our past and less likely to think through the moment. A little self-awareness can go a long way to help you understand any mindset that isn't working for you or any behaviours you wish to change.

Do you pay attention to your thoughts or take time to notice your emotions in a moment of doubt or a tricky conversation? This exercise can be a powerful and helpful strategy that can assist us in feeling and being more in control at difficult times. It is essential because we have thousands of thoughts running through our mind through the course of a day, with an overwhelming majority being negative.

Self-reflection is a powerful tool to help us maintain our composure. By keeping an eye on yourself, almost like a curious observer, it helps you to keep your attention at the moment where you have the most control. It is also important to remember that there will be times when we don't react in our preferred way. That we may raise our voice, say something unkind or do something we regret. Notice that and see this for what it is – an opportunity for you to show your child that you are human.

> 'I'm sorry that I raised my voice at you. I was feeling frustrated, and I took it out on you. I've had a rough day today. A few things didn't go as planned, and I had lunch on the run. I need you all to give me some space this afternoon while I get myself sorted.'

your child as a mirror

Have you ever found yourself doing or saying something and thinking, 'I sounded just like Mum/Dad'? It's so common, so we shouldn't be surprised when it happens! Earlier I wrote about us as role models for our children, so is it any wonder that those who raised you were significant role models in your life? There will be times when you emulate their behaviour with very little thought.

I invite you to consider that sometimes the behaviours that we see in our children that frustrate or annoy us, may, be a mirror being held up to us. What is it in them, that perhaps you don't like about yourself? Again, this is an instance where self-reflection can be useful, and some honesty can be the best way forward. 'I've noticed that sometimes we both don't do our stretches as the physio suggested. How about we find a way to do them together to make us more accountable?'

Be grateful for the mirror your child will hold up to you and be willing to see what's inside it!

same but different

An important consideration is the family dynamic around sporting participation. How active parents are themselves and how much they are involved in their children's sport are essential factors in participation. Parents frequently ask how to manage differences in interests amongst their children and how to manage sport, particularly if one child is excelling within a sport and another isn't. The worry that a parent may be 'playing favourites' is often expressed, and a frequent complaint of siblings.

Interesting findings from sibling research demonstrate that:
- elite athletes more commonly have a sibling, with many studies suggesting birth order may be influential
- a natural rivalry may be especially present when siblings compete against each other in sport
- coaches benefit from being aware of the ways siblings influence each other, and finding strategies to encourage individual success are crucial.

In describing her childhood with older brother Robert, Suzy Batkovic recalled the efforts her parents went to, to ensure equity for her and her brother. This was particularly important when Suzy's success in basketball started to emerge, and considerable time and expense was being focused on her commitments.

> 'Mum used to keep track of all the money she spent and the time driving me to practice and games. She would always make sure that my brother got time and the same amount of money spent on him. I can remember it used to bug me when Mum would buy him stuff. She'd always say that she'd spent the money on me and she was just keeping it fair. Eventually, I realised she didn't want to favour either of us and wanted us to both have equal opportunities, even

if those opportunities were different. We were lucky to have great parents'.

The advice to parents concerning your children is to:
- Avoid direct comparisons
- Encourage and celebrate the differences in your children in sport (or other activities)
- Seek equity between your children, particularly when their pursuits are different.
- Aim for fair, rather than equal.

social media trap

Would it surprise you to know that more than 90% of two-year-old's and 80% of babies already have an online presence? With the ease in which we can place images into social media, we may do so with relatively little thought to the consequences of posting. If asking your child questions about sport tells them your values; your social media posts and comments shout your values to the world.

If the posts you share in relation to your child's sport tells their placings and successes, then *outcome* is the value you are emphasising. Not only to your family and friends but also your child when the day comes that they see your posts.

It's wonderful that you are proud of your child's achievements and perhaps it's an opportunity to share with family and friends who are far away. I'm not going to tell you whether to post or not. I will, however, encourage you to think about:

- your child's digital footprint
- what privacy issues are you violating (sporting teams, school, friends)
- you don't have informed consent from your child to post on their behalf.

Interestingly in France, both parents must agree to a post before it can be shared. Further, if a French child opposes the post in future years, they can sue the parent with a current penalty of €45,000 and one year imprisonment.

That is certainly something to think about!

the roller-coaster of discipline

Sports allows us to develop and maintain discipline. A challenge for parents can be disciplining through the teen years. Whether it be sports or life related, knowing when to hold our ground and what to do if they push back is essential.

The first thing to understand is that our teens have needs and expectations from us about discipline. Few teens will ever say that they want us to be tough on them. However, in many cases, this is what they need. An important mantra I have held on to throughout my parenting years (and now apply this in all of my professional and personal relationships) are the words, 'We teach people how to treat us'.

Suppose there is someone in your life, who is treating, you in a way that you do not like. I would challenge you to repeat those words and ask yourself, 'What is it that I am doing that is allowing this to happen?' Before we turn our focus to the other person, we need to hold up the mirror and turn it on to ourselves. Often, by changing our behaviour, we can change the behaviours of others.

The question 'How do you stay consistent in disciplining teens?' is one I often hear. For this, I rely on an analogy to keep me focused and consistent.

Imagine taking a ride on a roller-coaster. In part, because living with a teen can feel like a fast ride with lots of ups and downs! Remember what it's like to ride in a roller-coaster? With anticipation, you, place yourself in the carriage, and an attendant comes along and puts the safety bar in place. What do you do next? Do you sit there and assume its ok? No, you place your hands on the bar, and you push it. You pull it. You make sure it's going to stay in place. Why? You want to make sure it's going to keep you safe. You test it. That's what our kids do to us. We are their safety bar, and they are relying on us (in part) to keep them safe.

While our rules can be 'boring', and we may not always want them to do what they want to do, ultimately, they know it is the responsibility of their parents to keep them safe.

Our role is to be as stable and secure as the safety bar on the roller-coaster. When I am experiencing push back from a teen in my life, I remind myself that deep down, they want me to keep them safe – mainly to keep my resolve, particularly if they tell me that I am ruining their life!

Bring those two pieces of advice together: *we teach people how to treat us*, and *we have a responsibility as the safety bar in our children's lives*. I need to show my teens that I will do what I need to do (however unpopular) to keep them safe. Further, I will understand when they 'test the safety bar' and be consistent in my responses to them.

the SIX words your child needs to hear you say

When they walk off the court, leave the track, climb out of the pool, exit the arena or come down off the horse, there are six powerful words that you can say to your child.

These words will alleviate the pressure, help to maintain a helpful focus, and most importantly, tell your child what is important: your relationship.

Are you ready?

Smile, and say:

> I
> love
> to
> watch
> you
> play

aeroplane safety briefing

By far, this is one of my favourite pieces of advice and one I remind myself of regularly. I often think about it and usually find some way to weave it into the presentations I give, no matter who the audience is, because I think it's gold. It's undoubtedly great advice for us as parents.

When you travel by plane and the aircraft is taxiing towards take-off, the crew will take you through the safety demonstration. The typical script is:

> 'In the event of unexpected turbulence, masks will drop from the ceiling. Pull-on the mask, to commence the flow of oxygen and ... (and this is the gold) ... place your mask on yourself before looking after others.'

Put your mask on yourself before looking after others. You cannot look after others without oxygen (literally). You also can't care for others if you always put your energy into everyone else and never look after you.

As a role model to your children, they must see you take time for you. That you prioritise yourself and that there are times when your needs are placed in front of theirs. Finally, as a human, you deserve that simply because you deserve it. Look after you, remember the oxygen mask in whatever form that takes for you.

ON THE SIDELINE: RESPECT FOR ALL

CHAPTER 9

> A good coach improves your game. A great coach improves your life.
>
> **Michael Josephson**

COACHES HAVE AN ESSENTIAL role in the development of character and encouraging discipline for young athletes. In addition to this task, athletes need to have a coach who has technical and tactical knowledge of the sport they are coaching; that is a given. However, we also need coaches who have skills in helping develop the self-identity, self-motivation and positive thinking in individuals. There is a great deal of responsibility on the shoulders of our coaches, and when a parent can work alongside a coach, there is potential for significant gains by our children.

In an ideal situation, the coach can build positive relationships, is emotionally intelligent and emotionally stable to manage all the conditions that sport with young people inevitably presents.

communication is key

Open communication with a coach works best, and I am a big fan of coaches who find a way to communicate with parents as to:
- their expectations in-game and training
- their coaching philosophy
- intentions with regards to playing time (if relevant)
- the influence of attendance at practice
- what they want parents to do if they have a query or concern.

So how can you best support your child's coach so that they can help your child? The below suggestions are by no means an exhaustive list; however, it is consistent with what coaches have told me over the years. Above all, I would recommend you have a healthy dialogue with your child's coach and at some point, have a conversation with them to establish the expectations.

Parents to be a role model. Coaches want you to behave consistently with how we expect your child to behave. A further reminder that your words and your actions speak volumes.

Parents who are supportive and positive. Mood is contagious, so your support for your child and seeking out the good from the experience is essential.

Parents who encourage their child. 'Encouragement' can be a broad term! I have seen some parents scream negatively at their child only to defend their actions behind the screen of 'I am just encouraging them'. Encouragement might be about esteem, 'Well done, you're playing well' or perseverance, 'Keep going, you'll get there', or instrumental, 'Well done, here have a drink'.

Parents who are having fun. Smile. That's a great start! Notice what is enjoyable about your child participating in the sport that they love and be grateful for that opportunity.

Parents who cheer for both teams. Have you ever sat in the grandstands while your child's team is on the receiving end of a horrible scoreline, only to have the parents of the opposition team dance and carry-on like they are at a party? It's awful. Celebrate with grace and humility and encourage the opposition and give them recognition and encouragement in the moments that it's appropriate.

Parents who are interested and engaged. My sons both referee touch football. After some games they want to tell me in great detail and with much animation what happened play by play. I have minimal idea of what they are talking about. I don't know the intricacies of the rules to the level they do, and so it's not a conversation I can contribute much to. However, in front of me is one of my children eagerly wanting to share with me something they are passionate about. If you've ever spent time with a disinterested teen, embrace these moments of enthusiasm when they come. Be interested, ask questions. The content matters FAR less than the conversation.

Parents who are willing to help. If there is a way you can help to support the coach, the team or your athlete and you can, then take that opportunity. Coaching can feel a lonely job and so if you can offer your assistance or provide it when requested that will go a long way. I can remember one year in junior football we had a coach who would designate an 'assistant' coach. It would be a different parent each week and would stand down the far end with our goalie (also rotated each week). The coach was clear with the level of support that was needed by the parent to help the player. The goalie position rotated each week through the team, and by some marvellous coincidence, the 'assistant coach' was never the goalie's parent!

Parents who listen to the coach. This forms a basis for mutual respect. You may not always agree, but giving the honour of looking and seeking to understand the intent of the coach's message is essential.

Parents who don't shout at their child during games. Certainly, cheer, but yelling at your child is rarely helpful. You may also be sending a message that is contrary to that of the coach.

Parents who abide by the rules. If you are asked to leave a competition or a venue, then something has undoubtedly gone pear-shaped. The rules are in place to keep everyone safe and respected, so if you are crossing this line, it is time for some self-reflection.

Parents who don't overpressure their child. We have covered this in earlier chapters. High pressure rarely results in high performance in children. Be mindful of your expectations being passed on to your child. It is rarely helpful.

Parents who are smiling. ☺ Smile, it will relax you, improve your mood, and make you more attractive!

Parents who support the decision of the coach. Coaches, at times, have to make unpopular decisions. Sometimes these do not go in favour of our child. Our child might get less playing time; our child might have a deficiency pointed out. Whatever it is, if we know the coach has the best intention of our children, it is essential to support their decision without us undermining it.

Parents who listen to their child. To be heard is profoundly healing. This is a fundamental principle of counselling; it is the first thing we are taught. Listen to understand, and all of your relationships will improve. People value good listeners, so work on this skill. It significantly enhances your relationship with your child if you listen to them more.

Parents who respect the coach. Coaches choose to coach because they generally both love the sport and love working with kids and teens. When you can form a relationship with your child's coach, you set up an excellent partnership for the sake of your child.

Parents who respect the referee. Sport doesn't happen without officials. Humans, by their nature, will make mistakes, and so it is the reaction we have when we are on the receiving end of an error that reveals our character. This is particularly the case if you never put yourself out into the arena with a whistle in your mouth. REFspect for our referees is incredibly important.

Parents who know they are not the coach. If you are not the coach, you are not the coach. It doesn't help anyone, particularly your child if you start acting like you are. Your child needs you to be the soft place to land, remember your role.

Parents who don't argue with other parents. Our children's sport is not a venue for us to stage conflict. If there is a conflict and it genuinely deserves further attention, suggest to the other parent that you have the conversation elsewhere, at another time. Chances are it will allow everyone to calm down too!

For a downloadable version of these points, visit https://www.drjolukins.com/in-the-grandstands

when something goes wrong

There will be times when different points of view arise between either the coach and your child or you and the coach. What is the best way to manage this situation?

Communication and timing. A big part of the solution is to understand the role of communication and the importance of timing. Whenever you can, raise the issue before it escalates. A coach will much prefer a civil conversation than a yelling match. Timing is essential. A discussion with a coach immediately before practice may be distracting and disruptive. Given you may not know the scheduling, flagging with the coach that you'd like to have a conversation and when would be the best time is a great start.

Trust. Trust is a vital foundation for any relationship. Trusting that the coach has the best intentions for the sporting experience for your child and whomever else the coach is responsible for is an excellent place to start. This is particularly important if the delivery of a message doesn't come across in the best way. A poorly delivered message may be easier to receive if the intention behind it is good.

Consistency. How you speak about the coach to your child, speaks volumes to your child about your respect of authority. Unless the coach is doing something unreasonable, the coach must have your support; otherwise, their influence will be undermined. Your messaging needs consistency with the coach. If you disagree with the strategy by the coach, then you need to decide if it is significant enough to raise with the coach, or just let it go and be at peace that if you were coach, you would do it differently. Therefore, if your child objects to say, a defensive strategy, I would manage that by acknowledging my child and reinforcing the message:

'I understand you disagree with the defensive strategy, but it's important to remember that the coach wants it to go that way. There may be more behind it than you understand at the moment. If it's bothering you, why don't you find a good time to let the coach know you have some questions about the defensive approach?'

If they decide they want to do that I would also help them to articulate their questions, 'Coach I don't understand why we are doing play x in a zone defence' will be received much better than, 'Play x is stupid in the zone'!

when you are the coach

When it comes to youth sport, around 90% of coaches of team sports are parents or grandparents. Individual athletes are more likely to be coached by a paid coach (e.g. swimming or track); however, this is not always the case.

Despite this being such a common occurrence in youth sport, the research is relatively small. Choosing to coach your child can be an enriching experience – but it can also be fraught with challenges along the way!

Let's start with the positives; one study compared parent-coached athletes with nonparent-coached athletes and compared the athletes according to anxiety levels. While the research had a few methodological challenges, it was clear that anxiety levels were no higher, nor motivation levels any lower for the parent-coached athletes than their peers. Both groups had an equal focus on the importance of fun.

Interestingly, as part of a research project in the United States, both parent-coaches and child-athletes held higher expectations for those child-athletes than for other children in the team. This is a common observation I have witnessed, where a parent-coach in their quest not to favour their child is tougher on them than others in the team. Those children may feel like more mistakes are noticed, more criticism is given, and less empathy is offered to the child of the coach. This is certainly a meaningful conversation between the child and parent and an essential consideration for the parent to be mindful of while coaching. In response to this, some children may rebel against their parent, adding a whole other dynamic for consideration.

The best advice to parents who courageously take on the coaching role is to separate the coach-parent part as much as you possibly can so you can treat players as equally as possible. Equity amongst your athletes is essential, and necessary for your child.

I recommend having a conversation with your child about where the boundaries lie between being a parent and the coach. I have known some parents to do this very successfully by using the car trip to practice and competition as 'the transition point'. On the drive to training, the conversations might arise to the upcoming session (but please don't if it's an hour-long trip!). Then I would suggest the conversations about training end when the session does. You don't continue a conversation about training with any other player after practice, so don't do it with your child. Whatever ground rules you decide upon, make them clear.

If your child commences a conversation with you about their sport, I would again be overt in the communication. 'Are you asking me as your mum or your coach?' If you are mindful about keeping the boundaries, clear and consistent, it will help your relationship in both home and sport.

Ensure you maintain conversations with your child about you being their coach. While it might be something they enjoy in their younger years; it may change as they get older or the level of competition increases. The more competitive the competition, the higher the opportunity for challenges to creep in.

No doubt coaching your child through sport can be a unique and fulfilling opportunity. You'll get to spend more time with your child, have a broader social network, develop your skills, get to know their teammates. It will remind you of valuable life lessons, it's an excellent opportunity for your fitness – and it can be a lot of fun!

be grateful

Gratitude is the most powerful of all the emotions in eliciting positive feeling. Remembering to express gratitude about your child's coach helps to form a solid foundation within the relationship.

Thanking the coach is an important recognition and acknowledgement by your child to the effort put in by the coach. Over time it will become part of their routine and makes gratitude a regular practice.

The other upside of appreciation is not only felt by the recipient but the giver. When we thank others, it makes us feel good. So indeed, it is a win-win.

IN THE ZONE: THE IMBALANCE OF LIFE AND SPORT

CHAPTER 10

I cannot make my days longer so I strive to make them better.

Paul Theroux

Train, Eat, Sleep, Repeat.

RESPLENDENT ON T-SHIRTS AND posters in changerooms and gyms, perhaps an aspirational goal but an unlikely nor desirable reality for most. Many would argue (myself included) that a life devoted only to your sport is unlikely to result in ultimate athletic performance. Just as you wouldn't place all of your money in one financial basket, the pressure that is generated when an athlete only focuses on their sport is rarely helpful.

Having worked with many elite athletes over the last three decades, I can attest that even those who compete at the ultimate levels of competition find benefit in stepping away from their sport periodically to focus on other pursuits. For a teenager who is still at school, this will certainly be a beneficial necessity.

is balance even possible?

It is often suggested to teenage athletes that a critical goal is to aim for a balance between their sporting commitments, study, part-time work, friendships, family life and responsibilities, and any other hobbies they may have. I understand the intent of that message; I do often wonder how successfully that is attained and whether in fact, it is even achievable.

The reality is that our young people have plenty in their schedules. I am mindful of the language we use around our teens, and one word I aim to exclude from my vocabulary is busy. Say busy three times out loud – it even sounds anxiety-provoking! The truth is that wearing a busy badge does not help us; in fact, it hinders us. When people are working, it creates an environment of rushing, tension and at times, panic. Teenagers no doubt have a 'full' schedule, however, to label it as busy is to push them into a life that doesn't help, in fact it hinders. When you rush, you appear and feel overwhelmed, unable to pricritise, unable to manage additional tasks and have a lack of control in decision making about your own life.

A meaningful life skill for our teens is to learn to plan, schedule and not overcommit.

Below are some strategies that are useful in helping teens to avoid feeling overwhelmed:
- ⇒ Use a calendar or a diary to schedule and feel more in control
- ⇒ Go to bed at a regular time
- ⇒ Say no to the things that don't align with their priorities
- ⇒ Discuss multiple commitments with significant people (e.g. coach, teachers) to plan for managing deadlines
- ⇒ Find strategies to 'switch off' when stepping away from training and competition.

Teens need a mental break as well as a physical one. Athletes are usually good at understanding the role of breaks in physical training. It's why they know they can't train for eight hours every day without causing an injury. For the same reason, they need mental breaks, to step away from what they are doing so they can return fresh. Explaining a mental break as a performance enhancer helps to emphasize it's importance.

flashback

Within my first book, *The Elite: Think like an athlete, succeed as a champion*, I wrote about balance and elite performance. One particular section within the chapter, Life Balance BS applies equally to teenage athletes, and I will include an excerpt here:

> The notion that life is a set of scales with one key element on one side and everything else on the other is a fallacy. The idea that these things should be perfectly balanced is both flawed and elusive. As much as we may wish to attain it, a balanced life is unrealistic and unattainable.
>
> Can you have it all? This question is so commonly responded to with a resounding no. I would be more inclined to argue more positively. You can't expect to have it all – at once. The key is to very clearly understand your values and your timing.
>
> Athletes understand this. Sport dependent, the window of opportunity for most athletes, is relatively narrow. In the sport of gymnastics, you are generally considering retirement by 20 years of age. In contrast, an ultra-distance cyclist peaks at around 39 years. The average age for setting a world record is 26.1 years. Examples of athletes making Olympic teams, such as Dara Torres who swam for the USA at age 41 years are rare exceptions. Only 1.8% of Olympians competing in London in 2012 were aged over 40 years. To pursue an athletic endeavour, most athletes need to start in their earlier years.
>
> Your pursuits and the decision to specialise will vary in requirements depending on the nature of the challenge. But here are some tips that will help:

- **Know your purpose** – what are you passionate about? Understand what brings you satisfaction or challenges you.

- **Make better choices** with your behaviours and your timing. Be wise with the scheduling of your time. If you work most effectively in the morning, use this time for your more critical projects. This is not the time to be trawling through your social media. If the last thing you do before bed is check your emails, and you don't sleep well, why are you surprised?

- **Consider the consequences of your choices.** If our life is a garden, what we tend to, care for, water and nourish will be the things that grow and flourish. If you ignore a part of your life – your health, partner, family or career, don't be surprised when it wilts.

A story that captures the lessons of balance and timing is *The Jar of Rocks*. A demonstration I used to give in my lectures and would invariably end up in a soggy mess at the front of the theatre. Thankfully, there are now videos to make the point much easier!

Large rocks are placed inside a glass jar, right to the top. The audience is asked if the jar is full; the answer is always 'yes'. A bag of gravel is then poured into the jar, around the rocks. The question is repeated, 'Is the jar full?', more nods across the room. A container of sand is poured into the jar, filling the gaps between the gravel and the rocks. Caution across the faces of the audience as the question is repeated. A pitcher of water (this is where it gets messy!) is poured into the jar, and the room can finally agree that the container is full. The students are asked to reflect on the learnings from the exercise. The most typical first response is 'If you try hard enough, you can always fit more in'. An interesting perspective on life! The second question is whether all those elements would have fitted into the jar if they had been placed in a different order? The key learning here is that prioritising the 'big rocks' in your life is essential – or else they will never fit in.

The challenge with the big rocks, however, is these are the more significant, time-consuming tasks so often avoided or delayed as they seem too big or too complicated. More often, we choose to fill our time with the sand and the gravel.

What are your 'big rocks'? What are your gravel and sand? How well do you fit the big rocks into your jar and how well do you attend to them?

If you wish to seek excellence in a domain of your life, you need to be clear on how it fits in and find ways to attend to it to reach excellence. You need to understand that not every rock, piece of gravel or grain of sand will fit in your jar. What you place in the jar, and what you take out – is a choice.

Dr Jo Lukins, *The Elite* (2019) pp. 89-91.

the rested teen

Have you noticed your teen is often tired? From looking bleary-eyed as they wander into breakfast, or grunting an undecipherable good morning as they roll out of bed to head to an early morning training session, fatigue seems to be commonplace. Sadly, sleep deprivation is the norm for many teenagers. While the figures vary, around 85% of teenagers do **not** get sufficient sleep to function at their best.

Late nights during the week, added to long catch up sleep-ins on the weekend means that irregular sleep is, unfortunately, the typical pattern. The general recommendation for optimal functioning is eight to ten hours of sleep each night. A common observation I hear parents raise is that they can't understand why their child was a better sleeper when younger, and now their habits have changed. This change is partly due to a biological shift in sleep patterns that naturally occurs during adolescence. The teen can often fall into a cycle of going to sleep later (11 pm and later) and then needing a later wake-up time. Of course, the traditional school system does not accommodate this, and teens are frequently attending school tired and certainly not optimised for learning.

Some of the consequences of deprived sleep are:
- Compromised ability to learn, concentrate, solve problems and listen
- More significant challenges in controlling emotions, including aggression, worry, sadness and anxiety
- Health consequences, such as contributing to acne and other skin problems
- A tendency to snack on more unhealthy foods which may lead to weight gain.

The benefits a teenage athlete can expect to experience from sufficient sleep are significant and include:
- Improved physical energy and mental stamina at school, practice and competition
- Better reaction time and decision making in high-pressure moments
- Higher tolerance to exhaustion during sport and an improvement in the ability to sustain higher levels of training.

Sleep is a topic I have discussed with many teenage athletes. I hear stories of difficulties going to sleep, staying asleep, sleeping through alarms and finding it challenging to get going in the morning. Sleep hygiene is the term used to describe the many elements for optimising sleep. When I talk with teens about their knowledge of sleep hygiene, I am always impressed with what they know. Having a consistent sleep schedule, creating an inviting sleep environment, blocking out light and particularly blue light are all strategies teens tell me will assist them to sleep better.

Teenagers understand. They know that sleep is essential, and they know their phones don't help them to sleep. Yet, as with all the things we 'know' but don't 'do', sadly knowledge is not enough to always spur us to make the better choice. Let me share with you one of the pieces of information that I have found incredibly helpful for getting teenagers motivated to put down their phones and get more sleep.

I share with teens a critical finding to come from the work of Milewski and colleagues with an athletic population that averaged 15 years old. That research revealed that athletes who averaged less than eight hours of sleep a night are 1.7 times more likely to incur an injury than athletes who sleep more than eight hours per night. When you consider those who averaged under seven hours sleep a night, the risk of sporting injury increased by 70% over the following 21 months. This was double that of those sleeping eight hours or more. I pause after telling groups this information, let them absorb it as I see the look of horror on their faces and then repeat it: averaging under seven hours sleep per night increases your risk of injury over the next 21 months by 70%. I then usually smile and add (with my best parent tone), 'I hate to be the one to break it to you, but your parents are right – go to bed'. They usually laugh, and then we discuss ways they might disentangle themselves from their phones.

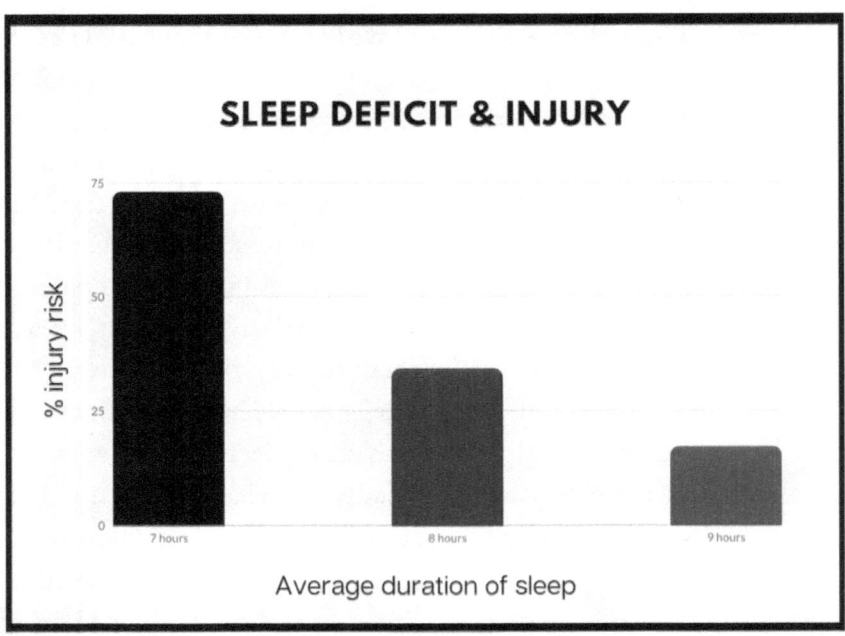

the electronic drug

When I ask teens, what are the most significant sleep disruptors in their lives, they typically all say the same thing: mobile devices. Our teens live in an environment where their social world is available 24/7. They can watch movies, chat with friends, scroll through the lives of others and dance, joke and summon all the world's knowledge any moment they choose. There are many advantages to our mobile devices, don't get me wrong – I use mine regularly too, and I'm writing this section as much for my reading as yours! Yet when it comes to the impact of smartphones on the sleep of our electronically wired teens – they are anything but smart.

These handheld devices stimulate through their digital content; also, the light may disrupt the body's circadian rhythm. Research with adults shows that the mere presence of a mobile phone near your work area (even when it is turned off) may have a significant impact on a reduction in your performance. In one study, adults either had their phone on the desk, away in their bag or in another room. Those who had their phone in another room performed significantly better. I describe it to teenagers, that if you can see your phone, even if it is out of the corner of your eye – it's like it is calling out to you, like a naughty friend trying to distract you.

My suggestion to you if this has struck a chord, is to consider that families need to have a mobile device strategy. I'm not a party pooper and very much see the advantages that mobile technology can bring to our lives. We also need to remember that they are highly addictive devices. When mobile devices are used unsupervised and unmonitored, it can make us antisocial, stressed, anxious and tired. We wouldn't give our teenagers a bottle of rum and leave them to it or set up an online gambling account and wish them well, so let's think about what happens when we hand them potentially palm-sized poison.

Suggestions for a family strategy for mobile phone use is available for you to download at:

https://www.drjolukins.com/in-the-grandstands. Discuss within your family and decide upon a family agreement.

Mobile phones and social media are a common cause of conflict within families. We certainly haven't always got it right in our family either, however, managing phone use and particularly its effects on teenage sleep is an important consideration.

strategies for better sleep

The tendency for managing teenage sleep by parents is to tell teens that they need more rest, they need to go to bed earlier, and they need to remove their mobile devices to do so. No argument from me. All of that is true. However, I am not a teenager in your household who needs to make the changes.

As with most things centred around our teenagers, this is the territory where telling (by parents) is far less effective than deciding (by the teen). Rather than arguing about bedtime, my recommendation is to have a discussion about the gains of a good night's sleep and help them to plan how to achieve it. Far better that they come to the realisation of the preferred behaviours and then we can assist them in making changes where needed.

A suggested plan for better sleep may include:
⇒ Discuss the pros and cons of better sleep (include health, injury risk, mental factors and psychological factors).
⇒ Suggest an early night on a Sunday night. This increases the likelihood of starting the week feeling fresh. It sets the tone, and it reminds of the benefits of sleep. Before Sunday night comes around, discuss what time that will be – leaving it until Sunday night increases the likelihood of 'stalling' and going to bed later than intended.
⇒ Work out the stimulating activities that disrupt sleep routine (e.g. computer games, social media, any blue light activity). Encourage a finish time for those activities each day.
⇒ Work out restful activities to do in the evening (e.g. reading, listening to music).
⇒ Plan out the week in terms of school, homework, training, relax time and social time a week ahead. It won't necessarily be rigidly adhered to. However, there is lots to be said for routine. Routine removes much of the thinking!

- ⇒ While planning the week, objectively consider the amount of commitment and review where needed.
- ⇒ Discuss the benefits of a bedtime routine. Sleep is not as simple and climbing into bed and shutting your eyes. Many people sleep much better when they have a routine. Habit is conducive to sleep; it also acts as a trigger to prepare the body to succumb to fatigue and go to sleep. The routine can start even as far as an hour before going to bed. It could include stretching, yoga, a bath, music, a soothing drink. Everyone's preferences are individualised. However, we all have different strategies that work.
- ⇒ Eliminate or reduce those things that stimulate you physically, such as coffee, tea, energy drinks.
- ⇒ Keep the bedroom dark at night. If possible, don't have a television in the bedroom. Think about the sleeping space, block out curtains, even whether the light from an alarm clock is disruptive.
- ⇒ Ensure the bed is comfy, the sheets are clean, and the bed is made.
- ⇒ If you want to gain more sleep and bring the time to go to bed forward, I would suggest doing this 10–15 minutes earlier for one week. Then consider bringing it forward another 10–15 minutes the following week. Drastic changes are less often successful.
- ⇒ Set a regular wake up time.
- ⇒ Substantially changing your sleep on the weekend can make it harder to return to your routine through the week.
- ⇒ Understand that drugs such as alcohol, tobacco and cannabis are disruptive to sleep.
- ⇒ If your teen continues to have substantive problems with sleep, consult with your GP.

IN THE WONDERING: Q & A

CHAPTER 11

> I never learn anything talking. I only learn things when I ask questions.
>
> **Lou Holtz**

ATHLETES, COACHES AND PARENTS within the teen sporting arena have shared many great stories that I have been privileged to witness and hear. This book has brought together what is lived throughout our sporting venues every week; children wanting to have fun and do well, parents wishing to support them and coaches teaching their craft to the athletes and weekend warriors of tomorrow. I will finish the book with some of the specific question's parents have asked. I have been mindful to 'tweak' each question to maintain anonymity.

What is the best way to help your child maintain confidence in their ability while keeping a balance of humility? Our son is very hard on himself, and his lack of confidence affects his decision making. He depends on his coach's encouragement which is not always forthcoming or balanced in our eyes. While we think he is fantastic, he doesn't take on what we say.

You've raised the important challenge in the gap that can exist between our belief of our ability and our actual ability. What is your usual reaction to your son when he expresses a lack of confidence in himself? Is it possible that he is seeking your encouragement? If that's not what's motivating his actions (it might not be) helping him to understand that mistakes are a firm part of the building blocks of learning about success can be helpful. For example, if your son was a goal kicker in rugby league, the only way to not make any mistakes is not to kick any goals! The message of 'every expert was once a beginner' can be helpful. As can noticing times when sports heroes make mistakes.

How do you continue to encourage and engage your teen at their sport when they seemed to have lost the passion/drive? I don't want to be 'that' pushy parent.

The first consideration is what is it that you've noticed in your child that has you concluding they are losing passion or drive? Then you need to consider the conversation you are going to have with your child about what their experience is. Tell them about what you've noticed and give them an opportunity to talk – and you need to listen carefully! The second sentence is something I also want to raise with you. If you are concerned about being 'that' pushy parent, then I wonder what you're doing that's made you think that? Sometimes the things we want to avoid are the things we are doing, even if we're doing it just a little bit!

We are having a problem with the coach. He seems to be a good sport when the team wins, but when they lose, he blames the ref, and at times his behaviour is embarrassing. I'm not sure what to do as I'm worried about what this is teaching the kids. Last weekend the team lost, and my son came off the court blaming the referee. I wasn't surprised, the coach had been yelling at the referee all game. That set off an alarm bell for me – should I say something? Should I pull my son from the team?

This can be a tricky situation when the values of a coach are different to your own. That being said, it sounds like removing your son from the team at this stage might be premature to other things you can try. I would see merit in having a conversation with the coach and remember that the timing of that will be important. It's also important to speak with your son. It's likely he might tell you, 'But coach said they were terrible too'. Here's where you need to manage a conversation around not all people share similar values and you want to reinforce what is important within the expectations of your family. I would explore all of this before taking steps such as stepping out from the team.

Watching the immense frustration and disappointment that my teen has endured, not being able to play the sport she loves for an extended period (12 months) due to injury, has been tough. Despite my child's maturity and high level of resilience, the mental anguish of not playing and despite considerable effort, won't recover faster by working harder is very evident. As parents, we have found that no amount of positive talk is helpful (the situation just sucks) and all we can do is offer a hug when it gets the better of what is happening. I can't imagine what this is like for elite/professional athletes, given that my teen doesn't have any high athletic aspirations, just a genuine love of playing sport. Are we doing the right thing?

That certainly sounds like it's been tough for all of you. You also talk about the conversations (and the hugs) you are having with your daughter and that is great. I am sure she is feeling very supported, if not frustrated. If you can normalise her grief reaction it might help her to understand that what she is feeling is to be accepted. Have a read through the injury chapter and see if some of the pointers for helping long-term injuries might be useful. If you continue to be worried about how she is managing, perhaps talk to her treating doctor, physiotherapist or consider if she might benefit from talking to a counsellor.

My son is a 15-year-old cyclist and performs well in his age group. The kids are great, but it feels like it's competitive between the parents. They are always talking about the latest equipment they are buying for their kids, and it's like they are all trying to one-up each other. It's such an expensive sport, and I can feel myself getting pulled into that pressure even when I try not to. Any thoughts on how I should handle this and not create an entitled kid who gets everything?

It sounds like you have a good handle on how this situation could go if you don't manage it! Cycling certainly can be an expensive sport. It is important that you keep the expectations and the equipment within the range of what is developmentally appropriate and within your budget! We do our children no favours if they are in the top notch of equipment from a very young age. In some circumstances it may even hurt their efforts and understanding as to the benefits of hard work. Wherever you can, leave the expensive equipment for when they are old enough to appreciate it fully, or even fund it themselves!

How do you make your kids clean up their rooms, not leave things on the new lounge, not leave empty containers of [biscuits/strawberries/cereal] in the [fridge/pantry], make them wash up after dinner without telling them to, and become champion athletes?

Darling husband, you can't. Get a new dream xx

My daughter is 13 years old, and I feel like in the last six years, she has done absolutely everything. Gymnastics, swimming, tennis, netball, soccer, AFL – it's like every year she doesn't want to go back to the previous sport and wants to try something new. How can I get her to stick at something?

Wow, sounds like your daughter (and you) have been exploring! Your daughter is doing what we would call in the textbooks – sport sampling. Sport sampling is moving from one sport to the next experiencing a full range of sporting skills, coordination and control. If your principal concern is that she hasn't found a sport to focus on entirely, can I try to put your mind at rest and tell you what you are doing is FANTASTIC for her sporting development? The recommendation for children her age is that early sport sampling may be the reason she has an even longer playing career, increased physical capacity and lower risks of injury due to a broad range of motor patterns. It can be challenging if there is an overemphasis on the competition during that time. For example – the soccer competition has a final series at the end of the season, and your child is benched due to lack of experience and becomes demotivated. The other challenge for you within the family is the possible financial cost of changing sports regularly. However, with the pace at which my children have grown over the years, it feels like I'm buying new uniforms every three months! So, to answer your question, if your concern is about not sticking with a sport for more than one season at this age, it is not doing her harm physically, and in terms of sports development may be what she needs! You'll just need to decide what works best for you as a family. I think her enthusiasm to try new things is a great attribute!

I am a parent of a teenage daughter who has high functioning autism and a particular interest in sport, especially swimming. What advice would you give her with regards to the importance of stretching and flexibility? She seems to think that doing it when she trains and competes is enough!

Great to hear your daughter has a particular interest in swimming. I agree with you that stretching is incredibly important. The recommendations by trainers reinforce the benefits in terms of mobility and flexibility. Many teens will prefer to do the activities they like and have probably not had as many injuries as us 'mature athletes' to realise their value! You mention your daughter lives with high functioning autism. So, this may be impacting on her relationship with stretching. I won't assume but acknowledge that might be the case in her situation. The best strategy I've found for teens with stretching and flexibility (and other things such as hydrating, getting enough sleep) is to recognise that success leaves clues. I tell them that when we pay attention to what works and we follow the clues, we maximise our chances of success. So, if I was speaking with a group of athletes about stretching, I might have them speculate as to what they think is the typical stretching habits of X (favourite elite athlete). Their expectations are usually that elite performers, stretch, get lots of sleep, hydrate, etc. and so I use them as the role model template, and that can be a useful conversation. I ask them to outline the pros and cons of stretching/not stretching and bring them to a place of making a decision rather than it is looking too much like advice from a parent (because they all love our advice!).

My teen is so serious! He's so focused on becoming a professional athlete what advice do you give teenagers about the importance of having fun at this age with their sport?

It sounds as if your son has a particular focus and has set himself aspirational goals. Both great attributes! I hear your concern that perhaps in having a serious focus, you are worried if the element of fun has lost its priority. One thing to consider is that enjoyment can take many forms, and sometimes what we enjoy doesn't always bring an immediate smile to our face – running a fartlek session is a great example! I would suggest keeping up the conversation with your son about what he enjoys about his sport. Listen carefully to what he tells you. Perhaps talk about an athlete in his sport who shares what they enjoy about training and competing – an Ash Barty or an Eliud Kipchoge. Teens need to understand that fun is serious business and is an integral part of the sport!

My daughter is a late bloomer. She is much smaller than other kids in her team and she plays in a double age group, so every second year she is tiny! Sometimes she comments that she'll always be little and never be as good as the others. I know she may have a growth spurt down the track, but maybe she won't. Any suggestions for how I help her to cope now?

It can be challenging to teach patience to young ones who feel like they will never catch up physically to their peers. Particularly as you don't know if they will or won't. It can be challenging as early maturers typically dominate in the early years. Then as teens hit their developmental growth, it becomes evident whether the early maturers also learnt the skills required to maintain high performance, or whether the stubborn nature of being the little one shines through. I have seen both with my sons. One started tall when commencing primary school, then was one of the shortest from grades 4-10, and now he pats me on the head. My youngest has stood in the centre of the back row of the school photograph since grade 1, we keep waiting for him to stop growing and it won't be anytime soon. The point is that children will mature at different rates and the ability to learn patience before they become discouraged is important. There are plenty of examples of successful athletes (from Jonathan Thurston to Michael Jordan) who overcame developmental difference to shine.

My 16-year-old son plays water polo. He's been playing for two years and started swimming squad when he was six years old. The issue is he is so inconsistent. Some games he is one of the best athletes in the water and other games it's like it's his first game. I don't understand how he can be great one week and not the next. Any thoughts?

In a situation such as this I would have a few theories about what might be happening. The first is that it is very normal for teens to at times be inconsistent in performance. Whilst all their preparation might be the same week in, week out, sometimes it's not as pretty as other weeks. To expect teens to perform at a consistently high standard all the time, particularly when they are still developing their skills and experiencing all the normal developmental changes of the teen years is a big expectation. Secondly, water polo is a challenging sport – it's essentially mastering rugby in water! When a sport is physically demanding and technically challenging variability in performance would be expected. Finally, it might be worth considering the amount of load your child is sustaining. Is he possibly doing too much? Is he on a path to burnout? These can be some of the issues to explain inconsistency. You could start by having a conversation with your child – but please don't say, 'Why are you inconsistent?!' Ask them how they are going and then see where the conversation takes you. If you are concerned you could also raise this with the coach, not from the perspective of requiring an answer but more for raising your observation and see what their perspective is.

IN A NUTSHELL: TEN KEY TAKEAWAYS

CHAPTER 12

The finish line is just the beginning of a whole new race.
Unknown

WE HAVE COVERED MUCH terrain throughout this book, and it is not my aim for it to feel too much or overwhelming. That you picked up this book and read this far says much for your interest in supporting and encouraging your teenager. As parents, we can only ever do our best.

In bringing together what I consider to be some of the key messages, I share them here as my top ten.

1. **Keep sports fun.** The leading cause of dropout is when sport stops being fun. Keep fun on the radar. Competition is the

optional extra in life. It is what children 'get to do' rather than 'have to do'. Having fun is the glue that keeps sport together, even when it is challenging, or the significant events come along.

2. **What's the plan?** Why do you want your child to play? Competition, friends, being part of the team, setting goals, learning discipline. Why does your child want to play? Be aware your goals may be different and factor that into your decision making. Acceptance of your child's motivation and sources of enjoyment is an essential realisation for parenting your child well through their sporting journey.

3. **Process over the outcome.** Winning comes from focusing on the process and enjoying the journey. 'Outcome' conversations can become a problem and a source of stress. When children understand that a positive outcome is a reflection of the process done well, they can shift their attention to where they have the most significant influence.

4. **You are a role model.** Your child (and others) are watching. Your actions reinforce what you consider to be appropriate behaviour. Children particularly can smell hypocrisy from 1000 paces! Be physically active. In whatever form is right for your body, be an active participant. You can't tell your child to get off the couch if you're not prepared to do it yourself. Demonstrate composure and poise in the grandstands. You need to be a good sport – for you and your child.

5. **Remember who is the coach.** Step back from the temptation of coaching your child. Over coaching can lead to mistakes and cautious performance. Your words can be confusing, require further thinking by your child and could even be

IN A NUTSHELL: TEN KEY TAKEAWAYS

contradictory to the coach's messages. Wherever possible defer coaching questions back to the coach and whenever appropriate, support the coach in their decisions (even if your child doesn't like it).

6. **Self-esteem.** Help to remind your child that they are a person who is an athlete, not solely an athlete. Self-worth should not be about wins or losses. Esteem is best enhanced through effort – something within a person's control.

7. **Your initial reaction is essential.** Smile. 'Did you have fun?' Your child will learn what's valued by the questions you ask. Say, 'I love to watch you play'.

8. **Understand the meaning behind your questions and comments.** What you say to your child after practice and competition will highlight what you think is essential. 'Did you win?' says that winning is important. 'Did you have fun?' places emphasis on enjoyment. Your questions matter.

9. **The curse of the PB.** Focusing on improvement is undoubtedly preferential to concentrate solely on the outcome. Be careful though to overly focus on PB. Mastery and development are a better focus than competitive rank.

10. **Be the soft place to land.** Sport comes with risk. Anytime you put yourself out there in a competitive environment, you run the risk of failing. Failing is ok. Failing is an opportunity to build resilience. Use empathy over sympathy wherever possible.

I trust this book has offered you food for thought and some practical tips you can use at home and when in the grandstands. Wishing you and your teen all the best!

FURTHER READING AND REFERENCES

Badenhausen, K. (2019). Behind the numbers of the top-earning athletes, *Forbes*, viewed 30 July 2020. https://www.forbes.com/sites/kurtbadenhausen/2019/06/11/behind-the-numbers-of-the-top-earning-athletes-2019/#c41d9b06bbed

Barber, H., Sukhi, H., & White, S. (1999). The influence of parentcoaches on participant motivation and competitive anxiety in youth sport participants. *Journal of Sport Behaviour*, 22 (2), 162-172.'

Brank, E., & Haby, J. (2011). Why not blame the parents? *Judicial Notebook*, 42 (10), 28.

Brown, J., & Wong, J. (2017). How gratitude changes you and your brain. Mindful. https://www.mindful.org/gratitude-changes-brain/.

Carette, B. Anseel, F. & Van Yperen, N.W. (2011) Born to learn or born to win? Birth order effects on achievement goals, *Journal of Research in Personality*, 45, 500–503.

Chen, L., & Wu, C. (2013). Gratitude enhances change in athletes' self-esteem: The moderating role of trust in coach. *Journal of Applied Sport Psychology*, 26, 363-376.

Crane, J.R., & Temple, V.A. (2015). A systematic review of dropout from organized sport among children and youth, *European Physical Education Review*, 21 (1), 114–131.

Gabana, N. (2019). Gratitude in Sport: Positive Psychology for Athletes and Implications for Mental Health, Well-Being, and Performance. *Theoretical Approaches to Multi-Cultural Positive Psychological Interventions*, 345–370..

Howells, K., & Fitzallen, N. (2019). Enhancement of gratitude in the context of elite athletes: Outcomes and challenges. *Qualitative Research in Sport, Exercise and Health*. https://doi/full/10.1080/2159676X.2019.1679868.

Pitas, N. (2012). Exploring the parent-coach and child-athlete relationship in the recreational sport context Masters Thesis, University of New Hampshire.

Robert Wood Johnson Foundation, (2015). Sports & Health in America: A Report.

https://media.npr.org/documents/2015/june/sportsandhealthpoll.pdf

Visek, A., Mannix, H., Chandran, A., Cleary, S., McDonnell, K., & DiPietro, L. (2018). Perceived importance of the fun integration theory's factors and determinants: A comparison among players, parents, and coaches. *International Journal of Sports Science & Coaching*, 13(6), 849-862.

To read more of Dr Lukins original writing on elite performance and its application for everyday living, visit www.drjolukins.com/shop (and use NOSTAMPS for free shipping).

ABOUT THE AUTHOR

DR JO LUKINS SPENDS her day inside the heads of individuals, teams and organisations – seeking to understand what makes them tick and assisting them to reach their potential. A psychological Indiana Jones, she describes it as a truly fascinating career that she is grateful for every day.

She holds a PhD in Psychology, has over 25 years of experience, and a breadth of knowledge in the sport, organisational and educational domains. She delivers programs in resilience and expert performance for the Australian Defence Force and has worked with elite athletes and outstanding professionals throughout her career, giving her a unique insight into the world of success. She has been acknowledged as an expert in her field, being awarded an Outstanding Alumni by James Cook University for her achievements. Dr Jo is sought after as a presenter, interventionist and for her expertise in the media space.

Knowing that she has made a difference in the lives of others is the 'why' of her work and the most satisfying element of her career.

Website	www.drjolukins.com
Twitter	@Dr_Jo_Lukins
Facebook	Dr Jo Lukins
Facebook Group	The Locker Room
LinkedIn	Dr Jo Lukins

BONUS OFFER

HAVE YOU EVER WONDERED HOW TO GAIN THAT EXTRA EDGE?

IN HER FIRST BOOK *The Elite*, Dr Jo Lukins reveals the 10 key secrets that enable elite performers to master their craft.

Download your FREE copy of Chapter One from the audiobook at: https://www.drjolukins.com/the-elite

If you would like to purchase *The Elite*, please enter ITG25 in the Promo Code to receive 25% discount and free shipping. https://www.drjolukins.com/shop

NEED A SPEAKER FOR YOUR SPORTING CLUB?

WHEN HOSTING A WORKSHOP or seminar you need a facilitator who will engage with your audience and deliver information and strategies that are practical and achievable. Knowing that the content is based on the latest scientific information and delivered in a personable and understandable way is crucial for the success of your event.

Dr Jo Lukins is a highly acclaimed and awarded conference and keynote speaker. Applauded for her warm, conversational style, her extensive professional experience is built on a foundation of academic knowledge. Jo understands that the key to a great presentation is an engaging delivery through stories and practical examples, with a take home message to facilitate learning and growth.

Positive psychology is the science of what goes well. With over 25 years of experience in the positive psychology domain, Jo's work focuses on wellness, happiness and success. From small group workshops to a full auditorium keynote, your presentation will be tailored to the interests of your audience to ensure it is interesting, engaging, and a catalyst for change.

Fundraising opportunities available for clubs upon request.

ONLINE LEARNING

So, you enjoyed *In the Grandstands* and wish to give your teen an opportunity to develop their mental skills for sport further …

Online learning opportunities with Dr Jo offer your teen a self-paced, flexible delivery option to further develop their mental skills in the comfort of your home.

Select one module or custom design a package to suit their needs.

- ✓ Build your confidence
- ✓ Elite sleep: Your secret weapon to achieving your goals
- ✓ Learn habits to transform your life
- ✓ Learn to embrace the suck
- ✓ Learn to use mental imagery
- ✓ Learn your recipe for success
- ✓ Mental toughness for overcoming setbacks
- ✓ Replace negative self-talk with positive self-talk
- ✓ Set SMART goals that will keep you motivated
- ✓ Staying calm under pressure

Online training offers an affordable resource to further building teenage mental skills. Each package comes with training videos, worksheets, and a plan to share with their coach.

www.drjolukins.com/inthegrandstands

NOTES

NOTES

IN THE GRANDSTANDS

NOTES

www.ingramcontent.com/pod-product-compliance
Lightning Source LLC
Chambersburg PA
CBHW021146080526
44588CB00008B/234